D0305768

# at home
## with
# amy willcock

# at home
## with
# amy willcock

180 recipes for every occasion from
the queen of Aga cookery

EBURY PRESS
LONDON

*for Jeremy*

First published in Great Britain in 2005

1 3 5 7 9 10 8 6 4 2

First published by Ebury Press
Random House, 20 Vauxhall Bridge Road, London SW1V 2SA

Random House Australia (Pty) Limited
20 Alfred Street, Milsons Point, Sydney, New South Wales 2061,
Australia

Random House New Zealand Limited
18 Poland Road, Glenfield, Auckland 10, New Zealand

Random House South Africa (Pty) Limited
Endulini, 5A Jubilee Road, Parktown 2193, South Africa

The Random House Group Limited Reg. No. 954009

www.randomhouse.co.uk

A CIP catalogue record for this book is available from the
British Library.

Editor: Gillian Haslam
Designer: Christine Wood
Photographer: Jonathan Gregson
Props stylist: Harriet Docker
Food stylist: Louise Mackaness

ISBN 0 091 90389 0

Papers used by Ebury Press are natural, recyclable products
made from wood grown in sustainable forests.

Printed and bound in Singapore by Tien Wah Press

# contents

# introduction

There are no hard and fast rules when it comes to entertaining, but whatever the occasion, the best events are when the atmosphere is welcoming, the company interesting, the food delicious, and the host relaxed. This is the critical bit – in order for you to be relaxed, you need to prepare ahead. This book gives you insider's tips, tricks of the trade and masses of guidelines to ensure that when your guests step through the door, the scene is set for an occasion to remember.

Creating the right atmosphere when entertaining is vital to put you and your guests in the right mood. It starts with preparation. This is the trick to everything in life – if you are prepared, you can do anything. You will have already decided what sort of party it will be by the invitation you issue – phone, 'at home' card or specially designed invitation, so you know whether the mood should be formal or informal. Seasonality must come into your menu planning and flower arrangements to get the best value for money and the best-tasting food. If I entertain at home, I use my table as the focal point and scene setter – an arrangement of country flowers from the garden and brightly coloured napkins and coloured glassware will signal that the occasion is informal, while a structured arrangement of hot-house flowers and white starched napkins indicates formal.

I've learned through experience that the most important element of entertaining is not actually the food or setting but the guests. A relaxed host, good food and a beautifully set table all help to create an enjoyable atmosphere which is what will make your guests feel relaxed. Agonising over your guest list will pay off – guests are what make your party live or die, so if you do nothing else, make sure you have the right mix of people at your party. Detail is crucial to a good party. So many people forget the little things that make their job as host easier. The main aim with entertaining is for guests to have a great time and that,

in real life, means that (you) the host will probably have worked very hard to ensure your guests' enjoyment and comfort.

Entertaining should be fun, not a headache. When I talk about entertaining when running a workshop or giving a cookery demonstration, I always say that if you want to really enjoy yourself and not turn into something Dr Frankenstein has cooked up, get a caterer! I know it is a case of 'biting the hand that feeds' to state that in the introduction to an entertaining book, but it is the truth! However, for the majority of us, it's simply not possible to have hired help on hand every time we decide to invite someone over for dinner, so here in this book are recipes, tips and ideas that will help you through the minefield that entertaining can sometimes become.

All the chapters in this book are divided into menus to suit different occasions and times of the year. You can either follow the menu to the letter or, if you are a more confident cook, swap the recipes around. Most of the menus feed six people, but many of the recipes can be doubled up to feed more. The recipes all have conventional cooking timings, plus additional instructions if you are using an Aga cooker. When it comes to choosing raw ingredients and deciding what to cook, be inspired by all that is around you. I know I have said it a thousand times before, but support your local farmers' markets and organic growers, cook and eat seasonally and, most important of all, enjoy yourself.

# essentials for entertaining

## party invitations

The arrival of an amazing invitation always sends a shiver of excitement through you as soon as you pick it up from the doormat, and makes a welcome change from the bills that normally cascade through the letterbox.

The design of the invitation will set the tone of the party. It can be anything from an engraved stiff card for a formal occasion to a hand-written and coloured design by a child for an informal do.

If you send people a written invitation, always ask them to RSVP. If you are getting close to the date of the party and they still haven't replied, ring them up and ask if they received the invitation – either they are just lazy and haven't put pen to paper or they are relieved that you did indeed invite them and, for some reason the invitation didn't arrive.

## domestic help

Call me old fashioned, but one of my dreams is to live in a fully staffed house. Sadly, like most of the country, I am head cook and bottle washer, although I do have help with the housework and, indeed, couldn't do the job I do without the wonderful girls who keep the home fires burning. However, there are times when we push the boat out and have help for a special occasion or really big dinner party. If you do hire help for the grand occasion, here are some guidelines to help you.

- Never take anything for granted and if you haven't told your helpers how you like things done beforehand, you have no right to complain. Remember: you aren't used to them and they aren't used to you and the way you like things done. Communication is the key to a successful working relationship.
- Always meet the people who will be working for you before the event. Discuss and agree money and uniform ahead of time. Check that they are insured; if not, check your own household policy.
- Take them on a tour of the house so they know where the loos are, where to hang the guests' coats; if you have a fire going, show them where to get the logs. Make sure they know where your stain removal kit (see page 15) and first-aid kit are for emergencies.
- Set out clear instructions about how you like the table laid, the drinks tray, etc. – basically how you run your house and parties.
- Make sure they know how to serve at table – food is served from the left, taken away from the right, and wine is served from the right.
- Explain your policy on how much drink to open and when to stop pouring.
- Teenagers are usually good at washing up as they are often short of cash and need the work.

## welcoming guests

Greet all your guests at the door – it's called 'working the door'. If you are entertaining as a couple, this is easier because one of you will always be able to do this. If you are the sole host, designate one of your guests (usually a good friend) to be on hand to chat and fix drinks for guests who have already arrived while you work the door.

This is a big part of setting the scene because you never get a second chance to make a good first impression. Before people arrive, make room for coats and check the loo smells fresh and clean and is well stocked with loo paper and clean hand towels.

When it comes to pets and children, I have both and, believe me, nothing makes me more angry than to arrive and have my brand new stockings laddered by an over-enthusiastic dog or sticky fingers on my dress, so make sure both are well behaved and out of harm's way.

Working the room is as important as working the door. If you are having a drinks party, it is essential not to get stuck or monopolised by one person. Always have a bottle or tray of canapés in your hand – this gives you the perfect excuse to move on.

tips

- Keep rooms cooler when entertaining, especially for drinks parties, even in winter – the more people, the hotter the room. A constant temperature of 65°F/16°C is perfect.
- As well as scented candles, incense sticks are brilliant for creating a welcome.
- If you find yourself having to make a speech and are unaccustomed to speaking, make it short and to the point and smile!

# setting the scene

I am not a great clothes shopper, but I do spend on things for the house. Tablecloths, napkins, china, silver (a big weakness!) – I just can't get enough of them. I scour the antique, junk and charity shops as well as buying new.

## tablecloths and napkins

I use good-quality paper napkins for everyday use, but when I have guests I use linen. I use the term 'linen' generically – a lot of my cloths and napkins are cotton. Never, ever be tempted to use polycotton.

White will stand you in good stead, so it is wise to invest in a set of white linen table napkins and a white linen tablecloth as your 'little black dress' of the linen cupboard. Perfect for formal dining, these can also be dressed down by adding coloured placemats or runners to suit a more casual occasion. I also like to use table runners as they can change a plain tablecloth instantly.

Invest in a waterproof flannel-lined undercloth. Not only will it protect your table when spills happen, but it also adds a soft layer, which feels great under the tablecloth. John Lewis sell these (see page 192).

When shopping for cloths, do keep the table measurements in your wallet so that when you spot a find you will know whether it is the right size. If buying a new dining table, consider choosing one that is about 76cm (2ft 6in) wide – I know that sounds very narrow, but it is a wonderfully social width that allows for really good conversation.

## tips

- Customise cloths that are not the right size for your table by adding contrasting fabric to them to make up the difference.
- To store your tablecloths, put them on hangers wrapped in a protective layer of plastic or cloth rather than in drawers. Label each hanger with a tag with the cloth's measurements so you know which table it will fit.

- When you are having friends to stay, you could ring the changes by using a clean tablecloth for breakfast and lunch, but at dinner use linen placemats or decorative hot pads/table mats if you have a wooden table.
- When folding napkins into a formal shape, always fold a linen napkin on top of another linen napkin – it makes a crisper fold and helps with the static cling.

## china

I have collected many different sets of china over the years and use them to help me co-ordinate the overall look for the table. I even have special Christmas china that appears from 1st December to New Year's Eve.

I can hear you saying, 'Yes, that's fine, but all the photographs in this book are on plain off-white or cream china, so what do I do with my dinner service that is 25 years old and covered with gold and flowers?' Use it, of course! The trick is to not put too much food on the plate – don't over-crowd it. Treat yourself to chargers – those are plates that can be put on the table as part of the overall scheme and dinner plates, fish plates, etc., sit on top. The chargers stay on the table throughout the meal and are only removed at the very end or after the main course.

You can collect very plain white china over time and use it for things like the main course, or use your dinner service dinner plates as chargers for a plain white pudding or starter plate to keep the theme going.

The main thing to remember is to use everything and don't just keep things for best because you will never use it, and the more you handle something, the better you handle it and it is less likely to get broken.

---

**tips**

- If you have serving tureens that are ovenproof, Aga owners can cook root vegetables in them. Bring the water up to a boil in a pan, add the root vegetables, boil for 2 minutes, then pour off all the water and tip the veg into the tureen. Add the butter and seasoning, then put the lid on and transfer to the Simmering Oven. Continue cooking the vegetables for 20–25 minutes or until tender.

- You may want to cut out felt rounds to stack between your china plates so that they don't get scratched when storing them.
- To polish china plates you will need a very hot cloth with as much water as possible wrung out of it and some distilled vinegar. Pour a little vinegar onto each plate, then quickly wipe it in a circular motion. The vinegar will polish off any residue grease. The plates won't taste of vinegar because it evaporates.

---

**glass**   I adore my William Yeowood glasses – they are old designs that are still made today, which means I can buy a replacement quickly and easily. The minimum for a formal dinner party is three glasses: white wine, red wine and water. You may also need other glasses for champagne or port.

---

**tips**

- Polish your glasses before you put them on the table by holding the bowl of the glass over a bowl of hot water so that the steam goes into the glass. Polish it off with a linen glass cloth.

- Buy a coloured china-marker. At a large, informal buffet party, ask guests to write their names on their wine glasses (before they are filled!) so when they put them down, they know instantly whose is whose.

---

**silver**   If you have it, use it! Don't keep it hidden away in a cupboard. I love silver cutlery and serving dishes and collect them avidly, and yes, I do use those special silver cloth rolls to keep them in – they really do keep cleaning to a minimum. The main thing about all silver is that it should be kept polished so that you will use it frequently, otherwise it will simply become a bore to clean when you need to use it and an extra, time-consuming job you can well do without.

**table talk**    The size and shape of your table has a big part to play in how sociable your guests are at table. Smaller round tables are good fun, but larger ones are distancing. If you have ever been to a wedding where you are seated on a large round table and stuck between two bores, there is no escape as the table is just too big to shout across. A long narrow table is best for keeping the conversation hot and flowing. Always seat people at the ends – don't leave them empty. The only disadvantage of a narrow table is that it doesn't give you much room for elaborate table decorations.

People agonise over seating plans, yet forget that the person seated opposite is almost as important as the people either side (unless the dining table is so large it doesn't matter), so bear this in mind.

**lighting and candles**    Lighting, like music, helps to create the mood of the event. Generally the brighter the light, the louder the room. For a drinks party your lighting can be bolder, but for a dinner party, start off bright, then move to a softer light – after all, everyone looks better by candlelight. If you have dimmer switches, use them. Mirrors are wonderful for bouncing the light from candles around the room. One of my tricks is to place a mirror without an edge on the table and put the votives and flowers on top – the reflection is fantastic.

I use votive candles a lot, and usually choose white or cream candles. I think they are best dotted around a table and the soft glow is so flattering to everyone. Always bear the safety aspect in mind, and don't place candles where they could cause anything to catch fire, such as a flower arrangement too close to a naked flame.

Only use scented candles in loos and sitting rooms – a scented candle in the kitchen or on the dining table can interfere with the delicious food smells. There are some special candles on the market for ridding rooms of smoky smells, but I usually prefer the open window approach.

---

**tips**
- It's easier to use an automatic stove gas lighter to light candles and votives than matches.

- A house should smell fresh so open windows and let the freshness in before guests arrive – don't over-do the scented candles.

---

**music to cook to and eat by**    Our kitchen is where we live, eat and entertain. One of the most important things about entertaining preparation is to not be too stressed so, while cooking, I either listen to the radio or to music. If you can, put a CD player in the kitchen or if you already have a DVD player there, you can use that.

Music is very important for setting the right mood and the best way of deciding what to play when is to divide the party up musically. These are my guidelines for the sort of music I like to put on for a dinner party.

**the cocktail hour:** Drinks are the musical equivalent of tinkling ice cubes so your music needs to be upbeat but not overpowering – try a bossa nova beat.

**dinner:** No vocals during dinner please! That high note always comes at the wrong time and guests will be vying for volume. Go for popular classical music.

**coffee:** You can have more fun at the coffee stage, especially if you move to another room for it. It is the winding-down part of the evening, so smoky jazz or easy-listening music is perfect.

---

**tips**

- A CD usually holds 35–40 minutes of music so you can work out your play list for the evening in advance and stack the relevant CDs next to the stereo.

- Movie soundtracks have some of the best music mixes so it is worth seeking them out – they usually feature tunes that most people know. But, of course, musical taste, like art, is in the ear of the beholder.

---

**smoking** If you want to keep smoking out of the house, set aside an area for smokers. You may have a garden, balcony or porch, which would be ideal. Do make them feel comfortable – a place to sit with a table with ashtrays and matches and maybe a pretty throw if the weather is cold. Some of my best friends are smokers and I have taken the view that I want to see them, smoke or no smoke, but my husband, who is an ex-smoker (the worst!), is ruthless so I usually sit on the porch with them and enjoy a smoker's moment.

**going al fresco** If your party is out of doors in the summer, consider getting the garden sprayed with a bug-repellent fogger. Also have plenty of citronella candles around and roll-on bug repellent for those who want it. Remove standing water (such as bird baths) from the area; however, the chlorine from swimming pools usually acts as a mossie deterrent. Make sure that your table arrangements include lots of basil plants as basil is a natural bug repellent. Bugs hate the pungent smell of lemons, eucalyptus and tea tree, so when laundering table linen to be used outside, add a few drops of these essential oils to the final rinse.

If your party is in the cooler months, have blankets, throws and pashminas at the ready. If you have space you could build an outdoor fireplace or, if that is a step too far, why not build a small bonfire on a cast-iron plinth – stack up a couple of logs and some coal, and there you have it. Think of it as a low-level barbecue. You could always use it to toast some marshmallows to accompany coffee!

---

**tips**

- Always have a wet-weather plan – it is a good idea not to invite more guests than can comfortably be seated if the heavens open and you have to move indoors.

- Light up pathways and steps for safety.
- If you have a fantastic view, make full use of it – even if it is chilly, put blankets and throws on the chairs to encourage your guests to sit and take it all in.

---

It may seem an extravagance, but if you are having a really special dinner or party, consider hiring a professional photographer. No one takes a picture like a pro and it will be something to look back on when the event has passed and all you have left is the memory. Black and white photos never date and always look wonderful, so do make sure you get them as well as colour prints.

Have you ever noticed how someone always produces a camera when you reach the end of the meal and the table looks like a bomb has hit it? If you want to take a photo of all your guests sitting down at the table, do so at the start of the meal.

When taking a group photo, don't stand like soldiers. Put one foot in front of the other and turn to the side with your body, but swivel your head and shoulders to the front. And whatever you do, don't put your arms around each other – it makes people look uncomfortable and fat.

# stain busting

At a big party, it's almost inevitable that something will be spilt at some point. You need to be prepared in order to treat stains quickly and every good hostess should have a stain-busting kit to hand. Don't panic but deal with it straight away and smile, smile, smile! The following guidelines assume that we are using white cotton, e.g. a white linen/cotton tablecloth. Heat can set most stains, so if laundering the item, wash at 40°C.

stain: grease
First Aid: Use warm, thick suds – squirt a colourless washing-up liquid on the stain, rub gently, wash and rinse.

stain: tea and coffee
First Aid: Stretch fabric over a bowl and flush with lemon juice and water from a height. If sugar is involved, flush with plain water and for milk, follow up with a commercial combination solvent.

stain: ketchup/barbecue sauce
First Aid: Scoop off excess. Sponge with cold water, then wash in hot suds and rinse well.

stain: soy sauce
First Aid: Start with water and colourless washing-up liquid, then flush with an eye dropper filled with a weak solution of hydrogen peroxide.

stain: protein (blood, egg)
First Aid: Soak in cold water immediately, then wash as usual.

stain: curry
First Aid: Treat as for grease (see above) and repeat if necessary.

stain: red wine

First Aid: Blot up excess wine quickly. Stretch fabric over a bowl and flush with lemon juice and water from a height.

stain: fruit juice

First Aid: Blot up excess, then use cold water to flush. Only use a detergent as a last resort as this can sometimes set the stain. Try flushing with boiling water from a height.

stain: wax drippings

First Aid: On solid surfaces: scrape up the drippings with a credit card, then polish as usual. On fabric: scrape off as much as possible, then cover the carpet or cloth with brown paper and iron it with a hot iron until all the wax is absorbed. Move the paper so that you are ironing on clean paper each time.

---

### golden rules

- Treat a stain immediately. Quick action is essential. Almost every stain is easier to remove when fresh.
- Remove the worst of it first. If you can sweep, scrape or vacuum it first, do so.
- Blot like mad – don't rub unless is it absolutely necessary.
- Use water as a solvent to remove stain in first instance.
- Pre-test – do a patch test on the fabric.

### stain-busting kit

Keep the following items together in a box for speedy stain removal:

- Scraper (such as an old, blunt knife)
- White cloths, for blotting
- Professional cleaning fluid
- White vinegar/lemon juice
- Brown paper
- Colourless washing-up liquid

---

## the larder and fridge

There's always the odd occasion when friends call by unexpectedly and you need to produce a meal at the drop of a hat. If you keep your store cupboard well stocked, you'll be able to cope with any eventuality. These are the items I consider my essentials.

**basic larder**

spices:

cardamom pods
cayenne pepper
cinnamon
coriander seeds
crushed chillies
cumin
fennel seeds
garam masala

juniper berries
saffron
smoked paprika
whole cloves
whole nutmegs (with their mace casings intact)
whole vanilla pods
(*I do also keep a few jars of dried herbs, but I generally prefer to use fresh.*)

**mustard:**
Dijon
English mustard powder

**vinegar:**
balsamic
red wine
white wine

**oil:**
grapeseed
olive oil (mild and extra virgin)
sunflower
walnut

**bottled sauces:**
concentrated liquid chicken stock
organic tomato ketchup
soy sauce
tabasco
tomato paste
Worcestershire sauce

**tinned goods:**
anchovies in olive oil
borlotti beans
chickpeas
kidney beans
lentils
plum tomatoes
sundried tomatoes
sweetcorn
tuna fish in olive oil

**flour:**
'00' pasta flour
plain flour
self-raising flour
strong bread flour
corn flour
potato flour
rice flour (*essential for people with a wheat intolerance*)

**sugar (all unrefined):**
caster
demerara
granulated
icing sugar
vanilla sugar (homemade)

**dried pasta:**
macaroni
spaghetti
tagliatelle
and any other shapes that please

**rice:**
arborio
basmati
jasmine
pudding rice

**nuts:**
chopped, flaked and ground almonds
hazelnuts
pecans
pine nuts
salted cashews
salted peanuts
walnuts

**dried fruits and vegetables:**
apricots
dates
figs
mushrooms
raisins
sour cherries
sultanas

**miscellaneous:**
apricot jam
Cheddar cheese biscuits
dark chocolate (at least 70% cocoa solids)
golden syrup

| | |
|---|---|
| honey | ready-salted crisps |
| mint in golden syrup | redcurrant jelly |
| olives in olive oil (black and green) | strawberry jam |
| organic chicken stock cubes | vegetable crisps |

**in the freezer**

| | |
|---|---|
| bacon | peas |
| butter | puff pastry |
| chicken breasts | roll of cookie dough |
| croissants | sweet and savoury pastry dough, already |
| Danish pastry | rolled out in tart tins |
| gold top milk | sausages |

**in the refrigerator**

| | |
|---|---|
| bacon | eggs |
| butter | mayonnaise |
| Cheddar cheese | milk |
| crème fraîche | natural yoghurt |
| double cream | pancetta |
| dripping | Parmesan cheese |

**in the fruit bowl**

| | |
|---|---|
| apples | grapes |
| bananas | organic lemons |

# the drop-in guest

Love them or hate them, they sometimes happen! What you give your drop-in guest will largely depend on the time of day they call. Mid-morning: coffee and biscuits; lunch: bread and cheese; afternoon: tea and cake; drinks: crisps and nuts, plus all the odds and sods you buy throughout the year because they look so good, such as olives: dinner – FHB (family hold back) and make it stretch!

**to make foods stretch**
- To stretch a tomato- or meat-based dish, e.g. spag bol, add a handful of porridge oats and another tin of tomatoes; check the seasoning.
- Add a tin of drained borlotti or cannellini beans or lentils to a casserole.
- Add more ready-made stock to a soup, check seasoning and add cream if it needs it.

My favourite stand-by recipe is risotto as I can usually whip one up with almost nothing. Just a few fresh herbs and some Parmesan and you have a dish fit for anyone.

## store cupboard risotto   serves 6

**handful of dried mushrooms**

**500ml hot stock, made from a cube or concentrate**

**olive oil**

**1 onion, peeled and finely chopped**

**salt and pepper**

**1 clove of garlic, peeled and finely chopped**

**285g risotto rice**

**1 glass of white wine**

**150g Parmesan cheese, grated**

**generous knob of butter**

**½ tsp thyme leaves**

**1** Put the dried mushrooms into a bowl and pour boiling water over them until they are just covered. Leave to stand for 10 minutes. Drain through a sieve lined with a piece of kitchen paper or muslin and set over a bowl to catch the liquid. Make the chicken stock up to 1 litre with the mushroom juice.

**2** Put a tablespoon of olive oil into a heavy-bottomed frying pan, heat gently, add the onion and cook until it is soft. When the onion is ready, add salt and pepper, the drained mushrooms, the garlic and risotto rice, and stir to coat the rice in the onion and oil mixture until the rice is translucent.

**3** Pour in the wine and stir until it is almost all evaporated, then add the stock ladle by ladle, not adding the next ladleful until the previous one has been absorbed.

**4** When the liquid has nearly all gone and the rice is tender but still has a bit of a bite, stir in the Parmesan, a knob of butter and the fresh herbs. Check the seasoning and serve with a green salad.

# my shopping secrets

The French are brilliant at buying tarts and other delicious goodies from their local pâtisseries (see page 192 for some of my favourite Parisian addresses). In this country we seem to have a problem admitting it when we do buy something rather than making it from scratch, but my rule of eating is – if you can't make it as good as you can buy it, then always buy it! I never make puff pastry – it's just not my thing, yet I always have a French brand in the freezer.

Find a local deli or food shop, try out their best homemade products and use them to keep the workload down when you're pushed for time. Mail-order food is now so easy to obtain – you can order it by phone or over the web, so get tapping and dialling. See page 192 for some of my tried-and-tested suppliers.

# virgin entertainers

There are some recipes that are so old that who knows where they started, but they are in the cooking repertoire of all women of a certain age. Everyone still loves and makes these dishes all the time, but you can't find them in a modern cookery book. Here are four quick and simple dishes (one starter, two main courses and one dessert) that entertaining newcomers, teenagers and young adults can master. If you are a first-time entertainer, these are for you. What new cooks need is confidence, and these recipes are fail-safe and tasty.

## sallie's starter    serves 4

**300g frozen prawns, defrosted**

**2–3 heaped tbsp really good mayonnaise**

**1–2 tbsp Greek yoghurt**

**1 tbsp curry powder**

**salt and pepper**

**lemon juice**

**4 hard-boiled eggs, peeled and quartered**

This is a great starter – easy and fast – supplied by my good friend Sal.

1 Rinse the prawns and drain them well. Remove as much water as possible.

2 Put the mayonnaise and yoghurt into a bowl and stir in the curry powder, salt and pepper and a squeeze of lemon juice. Fold the prawns and egg quarters into the sauce. If you like, you can add melon or mango pieces. Serve it with watercress and hot toast.

## chicken in mango cream    serves 4

**1 large chicken, cooked and all the meat removed and cut or torn into pieces**

**3-4 tbsp Worcestershire sauce**

**4 tbsp mango chutney**

**1 tbsp mild curry powder**

**350–450ml double cream**

**1 large mango, peeled and cut into long slices**

**salt and pepper**

You can also use pheasant, partridge, turkey or just about any poultry you like.

1 Pre-heat the oven to 190°C/375°F/gas 5.

2 Arrange the chicken in a deep ovenproof dish as the sauce will bubble up. Mix the Worcestershire sauce, mango chutney and curry powder together.

3 In a large bowl whip the cream to soft peaks, add the mango chutney mix and fresh mango and stir it well. Season with salt and pepper.

4 Pour it over the chicken, put the dish into the oven and cook for 20–25 minutes or until the sauce is bubbling and has started to colour. Serve with rice.

## honey and mustard chicken    serves 4

**300ml runny honey**

**1 tbsp Worcestershire sauce**

**3 tbsp Dijon mustard**

**1 tbsp mild curry powder (optional)**

**4 organic chicken legs and 4 thighs**

**salt and pepper**

You can use chicken breast for this recipe, but legs and thighs produce a tastier dish.

1 Pre-heat the oven to 190°C/375°F/gas 5.

2 Mix the honey, Worcestershire sauce, mustard and curry powder in a large bowl and add the chicken thighs and legs. Using your hands, coat the chicken in the honey mix. Pour the whole lot into an ovenproof dish.

3 Put it into the oven and cook for 25–30 minutes. Poke one of the legs with a skewer and if the juices are clear it's ready. Serve with baked potatoes and a green salad.

## pineapple and ginger cream   serves 8 (simply halve the quantities to serve 4)

**500g fresh pineapple or tin of crushed pineapple, drained well**

**4–6 pieces of stem ginger, finely chopped**

**1 tbsp syrup from the stem ginger**

**500ml thick double cream**

**4 meringues, crushed (store-bought)**

**1** Put the pineapple, chopped stem ginger and syrup into a bowl and stir well.

**2** Whip the cream to the soft peak stage. Fold the fruit and crushed meringues into the cream. Spoon into individual glasses or one large glass bowl.

**3** Cover with clingfilm and place in the freezer for 5–10 minutes, then transfer to the fridge until you are ready to serve.

# drinks parties

A drinks party is a great way to entertain a large number of people. See pages 126–9 and 133–8 for a good selection of canapé recipes.

**canapés**
Rule number one about canapés is that they must be tiny – just one bite per canapé – and not greasy. The best canapés are also familiar but with a twist. A drinks party is not the time to introduce things like sautéed rattle snake and flaming cocktails. You want the party to have an up-beat rhythm and be fluid. To achieve that, the drink must flow and the food be delicious but not challenging or messy. Paper cocktail napkins are a must for numbers over 10, otherwise use linen.

**champagne**
Champagne is a great mood enhancer. For me, it is the perfect drink. The bubbles always put everyone in a good mood and it slips down very easily. A fantastic way to serve champagne for a celebration is to add real gold leaf to each glass of champagne – the bubbles move the gold leaf up and down in the glass and it looks stunning.

**choosing wine**
Today many people seem only to serve white or red wine, but I think it is nice to offer a choice of mixed drinks as well. I suggest you set up a bar area and let guests serve themselves or employ a bartender for the party, especially if it's a big event. Check with your local hotels about hiring their staff for the event.

I also just want to say here and now that I totally approve of screw-cap wines and think they are marvellous.

The old rules about white wine with fish and red with meat still apply, but more loosely now. Do take advice from your wine merchant and drink what you like! I can't stress that enough. Don't be swayed by fashion – be true to your taste buds.

If you are going to splurge on the wine, make sure you have guests who will appreciate it as there is nothing more irritating than guests swigging it back and not taking any notice of all the hard work that went into the choosing and presenting of the wine.

The average bottle of champagne and wine will yield about six glasses. I would estimate half a bottle of wine per person at a dinner party. Allow one bottle of mineral water per person. Either use bottled water or have a jug of iced water. Please don't automatically put lemon in the jug of water or in glasses, but have slices in a separate bowl for those who want to help themselves.

# get-ahead entertaining

In general, remember the more simple the food, the better. Always try out a recipe on the family first. Not only will you know how to cook it but you can judge the timing better too.

To prevent high stress levels, write a timetable for yourself and a countdown to the day, even down to the cooking order – this is very useful for Aga cooks as the order in which things are cooked is different from conventional cooking. You will have to judge what needs the most heat and cook that first.

**menu planning and work plan**

When you are planning your menus, try to include things that are cold and need no cooking on the day, say, the starter or pudding.

Don't over-do the vegetables – you do not need two types of potatoes and three other veg. One potato, rice or pulse dish and one other vegetable are all you need. Look for recipes that are all-inclusive and have the veg already in them. I sometimes serve a green salad after a main course if I haven't served it as an accompaniment. It is great for cleansing the palate and for giving everyone a little breather.

**advance preparation**

You can cook a lot of recipes way in advance and then pull the whole dish together in a matter of minutes. It's the chopping and preparation of food that are so time-consuming and essential, but you can often do this all a day or two before. Clingfilm, vacuum-packing and zip-lock bags are your friends. (When you use clingfilm, do not be mean with it – tightly wrap the food in it, sealing it properly and trying to block out as much air as possible, as that is what causes the deterioration.)

When entertaining, I think some of the most useful 'tools' are warming ovens, warming cabinets and hotplates. And don't be hung up on serving food piping hot! Too hot and you burn your mouth; too cold and you lose the flavours – just above room temperature is best for taste and digestion.

**tips**

- Plates should be warm if hot food is going on them, but there is nothing worse than a hot plate for salad. Likewise a warm glass for a drink!
- If you run out of space because your cooker is full to the brim and you have a dishwasher, try running the plates through a hot rinse to warm them up.
- Onions are the only vegetable not to prepare in advance – don't chop them until the last minute, as chopped onion stored in the fridge will make everything else smell horrible.

# get-ahead vegetables

Restaurants have been preparing vegetables in advance like this for years.

**green vegetables** Have ready a large bowl of water with some ice in it. Cook your green vegetables so they are tender (about 2–3 minutes). (To keep green vegetables green, cook them in still mineral water.) Using a slotted spoon, remove them from the boiling water straight into the bowl of iced water. The iced water stops the vegetables cooking and helps them to keep their colour. Then drain well on kitchen towel and put into an ovenproof dish. Brush over a little melted butter or olive oil and cover with foil. Leave it in a cool place or in the fridge. Vegetables can be done in this way 24 hours in advance.

When you want to serve them, season with salt and pepper and put the foil-covered ovenproof dish into a really hot oven (the Aga Roasting Oven or a conventional oven set as high as it will go) and cook for about 15–20 minutes. Open the door and when you hear the fat spitting they should be ready. Serve immediately. You can easily do all your vegetables this way and group them together in an ovenproof serving dish.

**roast potatoes** Pre-heat the oven to 220°C/425°F/gas 7 or use the Aga Roasting Oven. Prepare the potatoes in the usual way: peel, and parboil for 5 minutes, drain and fluff up (put the lid on the pan and shake). Put dripping or other fat into a shallow baking tray and put the tray in the oven to heat up. When the fat is smoking, add the potatoes, baste with the fat and cook for 25 minutes. Take them out of the oven, turn them over and let them cool. Drain off as much of the fat as possible. Cover with foil and set aside. Do not refrigerate. They can be prepared up to this point 24 hours ahead of time. To re-heat, 25 minutes before serving, put the potatoes back into the pre-heated oven or place on the Roasting Oven floor. Re-heat and serve straight away. Timings may have to be adjusted to suit the size of the potatoes.

**frozen roast potatoes** Fully roast the potatoes and drain them on kitchen paper. When they have cooled, spread them out on a flat tray and open-freeze them. When frozen, bag them up. They will keep for up to a month in the freezer. When you are ready to cook them, spread the potatoes out on a shallow baking tray and bring back to room temperature. Re-heat them in an oven pre-heated to 200°C/400°F/gas 6 or on the Aga Roasting Oven floor for 20–25 minutes or until hot and crispy.

# oven-cooked vegetables

**new potatoes** Cooking root vegetables (or any vegetable grown underground) in the oven is so easy. It means you can cook root vegetables alongside the main dish while it is in the oven. A saucepan with an ovenproof handle or an ovenproof dish with a tightly fitting lid is very useful. If you don't have a lid or can't use the one you have, use foil.

You use this method with scraped new potatoes or peeled and chopped potatoes. The main thing is to make sure they are roughly all the same size and as dry as possible.

The ideal temperature is 190°C/375°F/gas 5, but if your oven is set lower they will just take a little longer. Cook them at whatever temperature the oven is set at for the main dish and adjust accordingly. For Aga owners, use the Simmering Oven.

For 700g potatoes, you will need about 80g butter. Melt the butter in a saucepan or dish and tip in the potatoes. Season with sea salt and roll the potatoes around so they are coated in the butter. Put the lid on or cover with foil and put into the oven for about an hour. When you check the main dish you are cooking, give the potato pan a shake. After an hour, remove the lid or foil and continue cooking for another 20–35 minutes or until they are tender and to your liking. Serve with the butter from the saucepan or add a bit more.

**carrots** The ideal temperature for carrots is 180°C/350°F/gas 4 (or the Aga Simmering Oven) but if your oven is set lower they will just take a little longer. Cook them at whatever temperature the oven is set at for the main dish and adjust accordingly.

For 600g carrots, peeled and sliced into batons, you will need about 200–250ml chicken stock or water (just enough to cover the carrots) and 40g butter. If using water, I add about a teaspoon of sugar and some salt.

Put all the ingredients into a saucepan or ovenproof dish with a tightly fitting lid and bring to the boil on the hob. Remove from the heat and, leaving the lid on, put it into the pre-heated oven. Cook for about 45–60 minutes or until the carrots are tender and to your liking. Check them from time to time. If there is a lot of liquid left in the pan, drain the carrots into a warmed dish and reduce the liquid to a tablespoon or so, then pour over and serve.

**frozen yorkshire pudding** Make and cook your Yorkshire puddings in the usual way. When cooked, drain them on kitchen paper and cool. Put them on to a flat tray and open-freeze. When frozen, bag them up, seal tightly and don't crush them when storing. They will keep for up to a month in the freezer. When you are ready to cook them, spread them out on a shallow baking tray or slot them back into the tin they came from and bring to room temperature. Re-heat them in an oven pre-heated to 200°C/400°F/gas 6 or on the Roasting Oven floor for 20–25 minutes or until crispy. Serve straight away.

# estimating food quantities

Assessing how much food is needed for a party is tough so here is an approximate guide. Funnily enough, the more guests you have, the less food you need to allow per person. It has to be said that I would rather have too much food than not enough, so if in doubt add a bit extra. The quantities below are for a buffet party. Puddings are usually best measured by the portion, as in each recipe.

**for 10 people:**

Ham and cold cuts: 1kg

Whole ham on the bone: 1.75kg

Meat for an all-in-one casserole: 1.25kg

Cooked, cold whole chickens: 3.5kg in total

Rice or pasta, uncooked weight: 600g

Raw vegetables: 1.75kg

Variety of cheeses: 500g in total

| for 20 people: | Ham and cold cuts: 1.75kg | Rice or pasta, uncooked weight: 800g |
| | Whole ham on the bone: 3.25kg | Raw vegetables: 3kg |
| | Meat for an all-in-one casserole: 2.75kg | Variety of cheeses: 900g in total |
| | Cooked, cold whole chickens: 7kg in total | |

| for 40 people: | Turkey: 12–14kg (the largest turkey that fits into an Aga is 12.5kg; for conventional cookers check the size of the oven before buying a turkey) | Whole ham on the bone: 6.75kg |
| | | Meat for an all-in-one casserole: 5kg |
| | | Rice or pasta, uncooked weight: 1.75kg |
| | | Raw vegetables: 5.75kg |
| | Ham and cold cuts: 3.5kg | Variety of cheeses: 1.5kg in total |

| incidentals: | Soup: 4 litres of soup will serve 20 people | Butter: 150g of soft butter will do approximately 40 slices of bread |
| | Sandwiches: 1 large loaf of sliced bread has 18–20 slices | Green salad: A large Cos lettuce will serve 4–6 people |
| | French stick: one stick serves 8–10 people | |

# cooking know-how .

To help you in the kitchen, herewith a few pointers.

**stocking the kitchen**

My kitchen is well equipped and I know from being in many domestic kitchens that so are many of my readers', but for those of you who are new to cooking, do invest in a few simple things to help you cook.

A *set of knives* you are comfortable with is essential. When you buy a knife, look for a steel that runs the full length of the handle as well as the blade and hold the knife in your hand to see if it fits – this is very important as the weight and grip are what make it right for you.

It goes without saying that *good saucepans*, *roasting tins* and *dishes* will make your life easier and your cooking more efficient. I suggest investing in a *large grill pan*, one that can be used over two gas or electric burners on a hob or in an Aga on the Roasting Oven floor.

A *bain marie* will be a huge help when making egg-based sauces and for keeping other sauces warm.

*Bake-O-Glide* is the cook's friend – not only is it superb for preventing food from sticking, but it makes washing up a doddle.

I have become addicted to *squeezy bottles* – they are cheap and are brilliant for positioning sauces just where you want them.

A *blow torch* is very handy for giving just enough colour to the top of a dish without fear of burning, but practice is essential if you want to keep your eyebrows!

Three big buys that will make cooking and entertaining easy are a *Magimix* (the little one and the big one), a *Kitchen Aid* and a *Gaggia* bean-to-cup coffee machine. I use mine every day and they are worth every penny.

## conventional cookers

Conventional cookers take a bit of getting used to. We have been testing recipes for quite a while now and the thing that I have noticed is how differently they all read. If you want to know whether the dial corresponds with the actual oven temperature, use a thermometer. You may want to consider buying a food probe as that is the only way you can be 100 per cent sure that the food has reached the correct temperature. One thing that you will need to do is always pre-heat the oven. For fan-assisted ovens, you will probably need to lower the temperatures given by 10–15 degrees.

You will also need to get to know the oven's hot spots and, of course, make sure tins fit – this is especially true when cooking for large numbers. Bake-O-Glide can be used in all your tins and frying pans, but not over a direct flame, electric ring or glass element.

## aga know-how

For really in-depth Aga know-how, please read my books *Aga Cooking* and *Amy Willcock's Aga Know-How*.

There is one big rule in Aga cooking: keep the lids down and cook in the ovens – 80% of your cooking should be done in the ovens. Once you cook like this, you will never be troubled by heat loss again.

This is known as the 80/20 rule – 80% of all cooking to be done in the ovens, 20% of cooking to be done on the hot plates.

As there are no dials to control the temperatures, food is cooked by position and timing. If you think in those terms, adapting conventional recipes will become second nature.

## aga temperatures

These are the typical centre-oven temperatures:

Roasting Oven: hot – approximately 240–260°C/475–500°F/gas 8–9
Baking Oven: moderate – approximately 180–200°C/350–400°F/gas 4–6
Simmering Oven: slow – approximately 135–150°C/200–300°F/gas 1
Warming Oven: warm – approximately 70–100°C/150–200°F/gas ¼

**picnics and al fresco eating**

I do think it's true that food tastes better when eaten out of doors and picnics always seem to bring back fond memories of childhood – even having a carpet picnic at home in the dead of winter is fun.

## picnic essentials

You will need a sturdy picnic basket or bag to hold all the cutlery, glasses, cups, salt, pepper, sugar, plates, napkins and tablecloth, plus a cool bag for transporting the food. You will also need items such as a rubbish bag, sharp knife, tea towel and corkscrew, and a torch is handy – I keep one in the car just in case. Wide-mouthed flasks are fantastic for keeping sausages warm.

Remember to pack things in the order you will need them. For instance, don't put the picnic blanket and tablecloth on the bottom of the picnic basket – make sure they are the last things to be packed.

A damp cloth sealed in a plastic bag is good for wiping up spills, as is a roll of kitchen paper. Clingfilm is great for wrapping up anything you need to bring back. I also use it to wrap up the dirty dishes and cutlery.

A picnic at the beach is a piece of cake if you are equipped to handle an overdose of sun, heat or sand. Pack a large tote bag with plastic bottles that have been filled with water and then frozen; as the ice melts you will have a constant supply of cool water and they can help keep your picnic cool, too. Fill a spray bottle with a mixture of one part rosewater to three parts cooled boiled water or diluted camomile tea to spray on parched skin. When you return to the car, use a soft-bristled brush to whisk sand from your feet.

If you are planning to cook outside on a campfire, don't forget firewood, matches, firelighters and newspaper. Always fully extinguish fires before you leave.

## picnic tips

● Tape the corkscrew to the bottle of wine so you don't forget it.
● I like to use cane 'chargers' – simple, inexpensive woven plate holders that mean you can use paper plates without fear of the plate's contents falling in your lap.
● If you are eating outside, put fresh lavender or rosemary underneath the tablecloth so when your guests lean on the table their elbows will crush it, releasing the scent.

## keeping bugs at bay

When outside, there are a few organic things you can do to make sure your picnic isn't invaded by bugs and creepy crawlies.
● Flies hate vivid blue as a colour, so if possible serve food on bright blue plates or containers. A bowl of lemons cut in half and studded with cloves or pots of basil are also good fly-deterrents.
● Eat Marmite or garlic – the smell of these foods evaporating through your pores helps to repel pests.
● Rub fresh parsley over your hands and face to deter insects.
● Sprinkle salt around your sitting area to ward off ants.
● A glass of Guinness is good for keeping gnats at bay.
● Pour a drop of cider into a wine bottle to catch wasps.
● If children are present, make sure they drink out of a carton or cup with a straw so a wasp hiding in a glass or bottle cannot sting them.

# Picnic for the Races serves 6

Picnics centred around outdoor sporting events, such as horse racing or point-to-points, are fantastic fun. Soup is welcomed by all and is both easy to make and serve. I find the best flasks to use are those made from stainless steel as they don't break if you drop them. The tomato juice in this version of Bullshot adds body and makes it a more substantial mid-morning warmer. Alternatively, if you wish, you can omit the tomato juice and add more consommé. Pack a couple of salads and a selection of pickles in your picnic hamper to serve with the Pork and Apple Pie.

BLOODY BULLSHOT
PORK AND APPLE PIE
BLONDIES
COFFEE

## bloody bullshot

**700ml organic passata (sieved tomatoes)**

**3 x 415-ml tins good-quality beef consommé**

**15g brown sugar**

**juice of 1 lemon**

**½ tsp celery salt**

**Worcestershire sauce, to taste**

**Tabasco sauce, to taste**

**vodka or dry sherry, to taste**

**1** Put all the ingredients into a saucepan and gently heat it over a medium heat. Do not let it boil. Taste and make any necessary flavour adjustments.

**2** Pour into a warmed thermos flask until ready to serve.

**Aga cooking:** Warm the ingredients in a pan on the Simmering Plate.

# pork and apple pie

**PASTRY:**

**345g plain flour**

**230g butter, cold and cubed**

**100g mature Cheddar cheese, grated**

**1 egg, from the fridge**

**salt and pepper**

**a little cold water, if needed**

**PIE FILLING:**

**750g minced pork or sausage meat**

**125g pancetta cubes**

**1 onion, peeled and chopped**

**2 Granny Smith apples, peeled, cored and grated**

**1 tsp freshly chopped rosemary**

**4 juniper berries, crushed**

**1 egg, separated**

**1–2 tbsp Calvados (or cider or brandy)**

**sea salt**

**1** Put all the pastry ingredients into a food processor and pulse until they come together to form a ball. Only add water if the mixture is crumbly. Wrap in clingfilm and rest in the fridge for at least 30 minutes.

**2** Put the pork meat, pancetta, onion, apples, herbs, the egg white and Calvados into a large bowl and mix well.

**3** Pre-heat the oven to 190°C/375°F/gas 5.

**4** Bring the pastry to room temperature. Line a 20-cm round deep tart tin with Bake-O-Glide. Divide the pastry in half and roll one half out to line the tin. Roll the remaining pastry into a circle to use for the lid. Fill the tart tin with the meat and cover with the pastry lid. Seal and prick a hole in the top for steam to escape. Glaze with the egg yolk and sprinkle over some sea salt.

**5** Cook the pie in the oven for 20 minutes, then turn the temperature down to 160°C/325°F/gas 3 and continue cooking for a further 50–60 minutes. If it browns too much, slide a piece of foil over the top.

**6** Cool the pie completely before serving with a salad, pickles and chutney.

**Aga cooking:** Cook the pie on the Roasting Oven floor with the cold plain shelf above for 20–25 minutes. Check pie after first 20 minutes of cooking to make sure the top isn't browning too quickly. Move to the Simmering Oven for a further 40–60 minutes.

# blondies

**360g unsalted butter, softened**

**180g smooth organic peanut butter (preferably unsweetened)**

**560g golden caster sugar**

**3 eggs**

**2 tsp vanilla extract**

**435g self-raising flour**

**1** Pre-heat the oven to 180°C/350°F/gas 4.

**2** Beat the butter and peanut butter together until fluffy – this is best done with an electric mixer. Stir together the sugar, eggs, and vanilla extract. Pour the egg mix into the butters, sift over the flour and fold gently but thoroughly.

**3** Line a 34.5 x 24 x 4-cm baking tray with Bake-O-Glide.

**4** Bake for 20–25 minutes. Tap the side of the tin to release any air bubbles halfway through baking. Don't over-cook as you want the blondies to be slightly squidgy.

**5** Cool thoroughly, then cut into squares and keep in an airtight tin or in the refrigerator. Can be made 3 days in advance.

**Aga cooking:** Bake on the fourth set of runners in the Roasting Oven with the cold plain shelf above for 15 minutes. Tap the side of the tin to release any air bubbles and continue baking for a further 15–20 minutes.

*blondies*

# Picnic for a Night at the Opera *serves 6*

Every summer a group of us troops off to an open-air musical evening. The dress is formal, so the picnic has to be too. For smart picnics you need to choose food that won't break into pieces and fall onto ball gowns or down the front of a clean, starched white dress shirt. Remember to pack a few votives (and, of course, matches) in the hamper – as well as being useful, they will add a magical sparkle to your picnic.

POTTED SALMON

PICNIC CHICKEN WITH TARRAGON

TOMATO AND FOCACCIA SALAD

PEACHES POACHED IN ROSEWATER

COFFEE

## potted salmon

**200g clarified butter made with unsalted butter (see page 158)**

**blade of mace**

**good grating of nutmeg**

**pinch cayenne pepper**

**1 tsp pink peppercorns**

**good grating of lemon zest**

**500g cooked salmon, flaked and bones removed**

**salt**

**1** Put 180g of the clarified butter, spices and lemon zest into a bowl and melt over a gentle heat. When it starts to froth, toss the salmon flakes so they are coated in the spicy butter. Cook for a minute or so, but be careful not to let it colour at all.

**2** Divide the mix between six ramekins, making sure you collect an amount of liquid equal to the quantity of salmon in each ramekin. Press it down gently with the back of a spoon. Cover with clingfilm and refrigerate until completely cold.

**3** Melt the remaining clarified butter and pour over the top of each ramekin to seal. Refrigerate until ready to serve. Remove from the fridge 20 minutes before you want to serve. (To transport to a picnic, use a cool bag.) Serve with sourdough bread or a baguette. Can be stored in the fridge for up to 2 days.

**Aga cooking:** Melt the clarified butter and spices on the Simmering Plate.

# picnic chicken with tarragon

1 medium onion, peeled

1 bunch of fresh tarragon

a scraping of organic lemon zest
– just a little

80g butter, softened

salt and pepper

2kg organic chicken

tarragon vinegar

200ml chicken stock

**1** Pre-heat the oven to 190ºC/375ºF/gas 5.

**2** Slice the onion thickly and lay it on the bottom of a roasting tin. Chop half of the tarragon. Reserve 3 sprigs, then scatter the rest of the sprigs over the onion. Mix the chopped tarragon, lemon zest and butter together and season with salt and pepper.

**3** Lifting the neck of the chicken, lift the skin gently, easing it away from the breast meat. Be careful not to tear the skin. Take the herb butter mix and press it under the skin onto the breast meat. Do this until all the meat under the skin is smeared with the butter. Fold the flap of skin back over the cavity, then gently massage the butter into the bird. Season the cavity of the bird with salt and pepper and the reserved tarragon sprigs. Place the chicken on the onion slices and smear any leftover butter over the bird.

**4** Cook for 1–1½ hours or until the juices run clear from the thickest part of the chicken.

**5** Remove the chicken from the tin and set it onto a plate.

**6** Place the roasting tin over a high heat and deglaze the tin by adding a splash of tarragon vinegar and scraping up all the onions and herbs. Pour in the stock and reduce by half. Strain and pour into a jug.

**7** You can either joint the chicken at this stage or leave it whole to carve at the picnic, but either way, place the chicken on a couple of sheets of heavy-duty foil. Making sure the sauce can't escape, pour over the tin juices and wrap up the chicken and leave to cool. When you get to the picnic all the juices will have set like jelly – utterly delicious!

**Aga cooking:** Place the roasting tin on the fourth set of runners in the Roasting Oven and cook for 1–1½ hours or until the juices run clear from the chicken. Deglaze the tin on the Boiling Plate.

# tomato and focaccia salad

500g focaccia bread (store-bought or bake your own – see below)

500g cherry tomatoes

salt and pepper

1 tsp sugar

1 tbsp tarragon vinegar

3 tbsp mild olive oil

1 bunch of basil

1 Tear the focaccia bread into small pieces and put into a large bowl. Halve the cherry tomatoes, add to the focaccia bread and toss everything together.

2 Put the salt, pepper, sugar and vinegar into a screw-top jar. Put the lid on and shake. Open the jar and add the olive oil. Put the lid back on and shake vigorously until it is slightly emulsified. Pour over the tomatoes and bread. Tear the basil into pieces, add to the bowl and toss well. Taste for seasoning.

3 Transfer to a covered bowl for the picnic.

# focaccia bread

30g fresh yeast

550ml warm water, plus more if needed

1kg strong flour

30g sea salt

118ml olive oil

TOPPING:

1 tbsp chopped rosemary

1 tbsp thyme leaves

1 tbsp chopped fennel top

2 garlic cloves, peeled and sliced

sea salt

olive oil

1 Crumble the yeast into the warm water and mix until it is smooth. Put the flour and salt into the bowl of an electric mixer with the dough hook in place. Start the motor and slowly pour in the yeast, then the olive oil. Knead until it becomes smooth and elasticised. Don't be alarmed if it looks sloppy to begin with as it will pull together.

2 Lightly grease a large bowl and turn out the focaccia dough into it. Cover with a damp tea towel and put it in a warmish place for about an hour or until it has doubled in size.

3 While the dough is proving, mix together the herbs, garlic, salt and enough olive oil to slacken the mixture.

4 When the bread has had its first proving, knock it back by punching the air out. Line a large roasting tin with a large piece of Bake-O-Glide and shape the dough into the tin, stretching it to fit. Pour over the herb oil and, using your fingers, press the oil and herbs into the dough, giving it a dimpled effect. Leave the tin for its second proving and to double in size.

5 Pre-heat the oven to 220ºC/425ºF/gas 7. When you are ready to bake the bread, turn the oven down to 190ºC/375ºF/gas 5 and bake for 25–30 minutes. Check the bread after 20 minutes – if it browns too quickly, place a sheet of foil over the top.

6 Cool in the tin for a few minutes, then remove the Bake-O-Glide and transfer to a wire rack to finish cooling.

**Aga cooking:** Put the tin on the floor of the Roasting Oven and bake for 20–25 minutes. If the bread browns too quickly, insert the cold plain shelf on the second set of runners.

*tomato and focaccia salad*

# peaches poached in rosewater

**90g golden caster sugar**

**150ml rosewater, plus a little more for sprinkling**

**peel of 1 organic orange (peeled with a potato peeler)**

**6 peaches, peeled**

**1** Place the sugar, rosewater, orange peel and 900ml water in a large saucepan on the hob. Bring up to the boil and stir until the sugar dissolves.

**2** Place the peaches in the boiling liquid and turn the heat down to a gentle simmer. Simmer for 5–8 minutes, depending on the hardness of the fruit, or until tender.

**3** Remove the pan from the heat and cool the peaches in the liquid, turning them from time to time.

**4** Using a slotted spoon, transfer the peaches to a dish. Sieve the poaching liquor into a clean saucepan and bring back to the boil, then simmer and reduce until syrupy. Pour the syrup over the peaches and set aside to cool.

**5** When ready to serve, divide the peaches between six bowls and spoon over some rosewater syrup and thick cream. Drizzle a little neat rosewater over the cream.

**Aga cooking:** Bring the poaching liquid to the boil on the Boiling Plate. Place the peaches in the boiling liquid and poach in the Simmering Oven for 15–20 minutes, depending on the hardness of the fruit, or until tender.

# Foragers' Picnic serves 6

This menu is perfect for autumn days spent mushroom picking, blackberrying or, if you're lucky, hunting for truffles. Although it might seem like a lot of unnecessary bother, I take a couple of those small transportable gas rings with the disposable gas can – they are about the size of a good dictionary. They are simple to use and there is nothing quite like the aroma and taste of freshly made, al fresco toast to serve with the figs and Parma ham.

---

PARSNIP, APPLE AND CHEDDAR SOUP

FIGS WRAPPED IN PARMA HAM WITH GORGONZOLA TOASTS

MUSHROOM AND HERB FRITTATA

BREAD-BASED BLACKBERRY AND APPLE TRAYBAKE

---

## parsnip, apple and cheddar soup

750g organic parsnips, peeled, topped and tailed

1 large onion, peeled and roughly chopped

1 tbsp sunflower oil

1.1 litre chicken or vegetable stock

1 large apple, peeled, cored and cut into chunks

salt and pepper

100g Cheddar cheese, grated

1 Put the parsnips, onion and oil into a deep saucepan. Gently fry over a low heat for about 5 minutes so they take on a little colour.

2 Add the stock and apple and season with salt and pepper. Bring up to the boil, then simmer for 25–30 minutes or until soft.

3 Blitz the soup with a hand blender until smooth. Taste for seasoning. If it is too thick, thin down with a little more stock and reheat. Serve piping hot, sprinkled with the cheese, and serve with crusty bread. To transport to the picnic, pour the soup into a thermos flask and sprinkle on the cheese just before serving.

**Aga cooking:** Fry the parsnips and onion as above on the Simmering Plate. Bring the soup up to the boil on the Boiling Plate, then simmer in the Simmering Oven for 25–30 minutes.

## figs wrapped in parma ham with gorgonzola toasts

**6 fresh plump figs**

**6 slices Parma ham**

**50g Gorgonzola cheese, cut into 6 slices**

**chestnut-infused honey**

**rocket**

**6 slices walnut bread**

**1 garlic clove, peeled**

**1** Slice each fig down the middle, leaving the base intact, and put a slice of Gorgonzola between the two halves. Drizzle over a little honey, top with a few rocket leaves and then wrap the whole thing up in the Parma ham.

**2** Toast the walnut bread and rub with a clove of garlic. Place a fig parcel on the toast and serve.

## mushroom and herb frittata

**olive oil**

**2 large leeks, trimmed, washed and sliced**

**500g wild mushrooms**

**7 eggs**

**60ml crème fraîche**

**salt and pepper**

**½ tbsp freshly chopped rosemary**

**1** Heat up some olive oil in a large frying pan and soften the leeks. Add the mushrooms and continue to cook for 5 minutes.

**2** Pre-heat the oven to 180°C/350°F/gas 4. Grease a deep ovenproof dish or ovenproof frying pan with some olive oil and set aside.

**3** In a large jug mix the eggs, crème fraîche, salt, pepper and rosemary together. Fold in the leeks and mushrooms and pour it into the greased dish.

**4** Cook the frittata in the oven for 15–18 minutes or until it is golden and puffed up a little.

**5** Remove from the oven and cool a little. Slice into wedges and serve with a fresh herb salad.

**Aga cooking:** Put the leeks on a baking tray, drizzle with a little olive oil and slide onto the first set of runners in the Roasting Oven. Roast for about 8 minutes. Remove the tray from the oven and scatter over the mushrooms, stir a little, then cook for another 10 minutes or until they are soft but not mushy. Put the frittata on the grid shelf on the third set of runners in the Roasting Oven and bake for 15–20 minutes. For 4-oven Aga cookers, put the grid shelf onto the third set of runners in the Baking Oven and bake for 20–25 minutes. It should be golden and puffed up a little.

*figs wrapped in parma ham with gorgonzola toasts*

# bread-based blackberry and apple traybake

**FILLING:**

**65g flour**

**pinch of cloves**

**pinch of cinnamon**

**good grating of nutmeg**

**60g unsalted butter, cold and cubed**

**3 apples, peeled and chopped**

**2 pears, peeled and chopped**

**250g blackberries**

**125g chopped organic dates**

**120g soft brown sugar**

**60g caster sugar**

**a little melted butter**

**BREAD BASE:**

**8–10 slices of organic bread, crusts removed**

**200g melted butter**

**1** Pre-heat the oven to 180ºC/350ºF/gas 4.

**2** Put the flour, spices and butter into the food processor and pulse until crumbly. Transfer it to a bowl and add the apples, pears, blackberries, dates, soft brown sugar and caster sugar and toss it all together.

**3** Take each piece of bread and fold the sides up slightly so that the fillings won't fall out and you can create individual pie cases. Brush with the melted butter and press onto a baking tray, one slice at a time. Pile some of the filling onto each slice (the bread acts like a pastry base).

**4** Bake for 40 minutes or until the crust is golden and the fruit is tender.

**5** Cool in the tray, then wrap the tray completely with foil and clingfilm for transporting to the picnic.

**Aga cooking:** Bake on the fourth set of runners in the Roasting Oven with the cold plain shelf above for 35–40 minutes or until the crust is golden and the fruit is tender. If it browns too quickly, replace the shelf with a cold one or use foil.

# Tailgate Picnic after Ice Skating *serves 6*

OK, I know most of us don't go ice skating on a frozen pond, but it's the fantasy that was in my mind when creating this menu and wouldn't it be great – so we can pretend! This substantial picnic works equally well for a winter shoot or Boxing Day at the races.

CREAM OF CHESTNUT
SOUP

SAUSAGE TART

SPINACH PIE

MARMALADE CAKE

HOT CHOCOLATE

## cream of chestnut soup

1 tbsp light olive oil

1 tbsp clarified butter

100g pancetta, chopped

2 large onions, peeled and finely chopped

300g vacuum-packed chestnuts

300ml chicken stock

300ml double cream

salt and pepper

**1** Heat the oil and butter in a large casserole, add the pancetta pieces and fry until the fat begins to run. Remove the pancetta and set aside. Add the onion to the fat in the pan and cook until very soft but not coloured.

**2** Add the remaining ingredients to the casserole and stir it well, scraping the bits off the bottom. Transfer to a food processor or use a hand-held blender. Whiz it all up, taste for seasoning and pour it back into the casserole.

**3** Bring the soup just up to the boil and serve piping hot (or pour into a thermos flask).

**Aga cooking:** Cook the pancetta and onion as above on the Roasting Oven floor or on the Simmering Plate. Bring the soup to the boil on the Roasting Oven floor or on the Simmering Plate.

# sausage tart

**PASTRY:**

**340g plain flour**

**225g butter or margarine, cold and cubed**

**1 egg from the fridge**

**salt and pepper**

**ONION MARMALADE:**

**1 tbsp sunflower oil**

**1 heaped tbsp coarse-cut marmalade**

**2 red onions, peeled and thinly sliced**

**salt and pepper**

**FILLING:**

**6 good-quality pork sausages**

**60g fresh breadcrumbs**

**2 tbsp double cream**

**1 heaped tsp dry mustard powder**

**2 large eggs**

**salt and pepper**

**1** To make the pastry, put all the ingredients into a food processor and pulse until the mixture comes together to form a ball. Only add water if it is crumbly. Wrap the pastry in clingfilm and rest in the fridge for at least 30 minutes. Bring to room temperature and roll out to line a 20-cm fluted tin.

**2** To make the onion marmalade, heat up the sunflower oil and the marmalade in a frying pan, then toss in the onion and cook very gently over a medium heat until the onions are deliciously caramelised and thick. Season with salt and pepper. This will take about 10–15 minutes.

**3** While the onions are cooking down, pre-heat the oven to 190°C/375°F/ gas 5 and blind-bake the pastry case for 10 minutes. Allow to cool a little.

**4** Cook the sausages for 10 minutes or until they start to brown, either in a frying pan or under a grill.

**5** To assemble the tart, spread the onion marmalade over the base of the pastry case. Mix the breadcrumbs, cream, mustard powder and eggs together and season with salt and pepper. Pour this over the onion marmalade in the tart. Slice the sausages horizontally and arrange them on top.

**6** Pre-heat the oven to 180°C/350°F/gas 4. Cook the tart for 20–25 minutes or until cooked and golden.

**7** Serve hot or cold with extra mustard.

**Aga cooking:** Cook the onion marmalade on the floor of the Roasting Oven. With an Aga there is no need to blind-bake the pastry case. Cook the sausages in a roasting tin on the first set of runners in the Roasting Oven for 15–20 minutes. Fill the tart as above, then cook on the floor of the Roasting Oven with the cold plain shelf above for 20–25 minutes or until golden.

*sausage tart*

# spinach pie

60g unsalted butter

1 tbsp olive oil

2 onions, peeled and finely sliced

1 tbsp golden caster sugar

2–3 cloves of garlic, peeled and crushed

250g spinach leaves

nutmeg

150g Gruyère cheese, grated

150g Parmesan cheese, grated

1 tbsp breadcrumbs

4 eggs

80g pine nuts, toasted

salt and pepper

2 x 500g packets frozen puff pastry

1 egg, beaten, for egg wash

1 Heat half the butter and oil in a large frying pan. Add the onion slices and sugar, season with salt and pepper. Cook slowly until they are very soft and just starting to colour but not too much. Add the garlic halfway through – you don't want the garlic to burn. Set aside.

2 In another deep saucepan, heat up the rest of the butter and add the spinach and cook for 1–2 minutes so that it just wilts. Drain in a colander and squeeze out as much liquid as possible.

3 Tip the onions and the spinach into a large bowl and season with grated nutmeg (about half of a whole nutmeg), salt and pepper. Add the cheeses, breadcrumbs, eggs and pine nuts and mix well.

4 Roll out half the pastry to a large rectangle and place the spinach mix down the middle. Brush the edges with the egg wash. Roll out the rest of the pastry, place on top of the spinach and press down the edges firmly to seal. Slash it three times on top. Place the pie on a shallow baking tray lined with Bake-O-Glide. Brush with more egg wash.

5 Pre-heat the oven to 180°C/350°F/gas 4. Bake the pie for 35–40 minutes or until it has risen and is golden brown. If it browns too quickly, cover with foil.

6 Allow the pie to cool, then wrap in greaseproof paper and foil to transport to the picnic.

Aga cooking: Cook the onion and garlic as above on the Simmering Plate. Cook the spinach on the Simmering Plate. Bake the pie in the Baking Oven for 30–40 minutes as above, or in the Roasting Oven on the fourth set of runners with the cold plain shelf above for 30–35 minutes, or until risen and golden brown.

## marmalade cake

**275g self-raising flour**

**225g golden caster sugar**

**225g unsalted butter, softened, or baking margarine**

**2 tsp baking powder**

**1 tsp vanilla extract**

**3–4 heaped tbsp coarse-cut marmalade**

**zest of 1 organic orange**

**5 eggs**

**1** Pre-heat the oven to 180ºC/350ºF/gas 4. Line a small traybake tin with Bake-O-Glide.

**2** Put all the ingredients into the bowl of an electric mixer and mix until well combined. Pour the batter into the tin and smooth over the top with a palette knife.

**3** Bake the cake for 30–35 minutes. The cake is done when it springs back when lightly pressed in the middle and it pulls away from the sides of the tin.

**4** Cool in the tin on a wire rack. Wrap with clingfilm and transport to picnic, cutting it there.

**Aga cooking:** Bake on the fourth set of runners in the Roasting Oven with the cold plain shelf on the second set of runners or in the Baking Oven for 20–25 minutes.

## hot chocolate

**320g dark chocolate**

**100ml hot espresso coffee**

**pinch of salt**

**1 litre milk**

**2 tbsp sugar**

**2–3 tbsp rum (optional)**

**1** Chop the chocolate into pieces. Put it into a double boiler with the espresso and a pinch of salt. Melt slowly over a gentle heat.

**2** When melted, add the rest of the ingredients and whisk. Pour into a heated thermos flask. This can be made up in advance and reheated; it can also be drunk cold.

**Aga cooking:** Melt the chocolate slowly on the Simmering Plate.

house parties

I love a really good house party. It's a great way to entertain new and old friends at home. For me, to have a packed house full of young and old is my idea of bliss. One young army captain (I do like a few uniforms around the house – be they army, navy or fire service) has nicknamed our house 'party central' as we always number at least 15 for breakfast whenever he comes to stay!

It is great fun to have a house party when there is an event taking place in your neighbourhood, such as a ball or dance or a sporting event. When people are staying the night you need to make them as comfortable as possible. It's a good idea to spend a night in your own guest room to see what is lacking (such as a bedside lamp) and to make sure you have provided everything a guest could want – to my mind, hot water bottles are essential and make you feel pampered!

**sunday lunch** One of the nicest things about having guests for the weekend is Sunday lunch. I try to invite people not staying for the weekend as well, to add to the party, but as ever, choose guests who will mix well with those staying over. Sunday lunch is very civilised and rewarding. Doing the whole roast meat thing means that you can serve a lighter breakfast. Almost all your preparations for the weekend can be done in advance or as people always offer to help, it can be fun to chat to them while peeling the potatoes.

**the menus** All the house party recipes in this chapter serve 6, but you can easily double them up for 12. I've also provided a vegetarian main course as an alternative (or additional dish) for the Saturday night dinner party so you can cater for non-meat-eating guests. In addition to the vegetable recipes given in the menus, refer to the information on 'get-ahead' vegetables on pages 22–3 for accompaniments. As well as the recipes provided for breakfast, I also like to serve a bakery basket filled with good-quality, store-bought pastries.

# Spring House Party *serves 6*

### SATURDAY BREAKFAST
FULL ENGLISH BREAKFAST

ORANGE MUFFINS

### SATURDAY LUNCH
CRAB CAKES WITH CRÈME
FRAÎCHE TARTARE SAUCE

SPICED GRAPES WITH CHEESE

### SUNDAY BREAKFAST
SCRAMBLED EGGS WITH
MAPLE-GLAZED HAM

BAKERY BASKET

### SUNDAY LUNCH
CITRUS-BAKED CHICKEN
WITH ARTICHOKE HEARTS

GRATIN OF SPRING
VEGETABLES

CUSTARD TART

### FRIDAY NIGHT SUPPER
SOUP AU PISTOU WITH
PARMESAN

SALAMI BREAD

PISTACHIO AND ALMOND
CAKE

### SATURDAY NIGHT
### DINNER PARTY
ASPARAGUS WITH BLOOD ORANGE
HOLLANDAISE

HERBED ROAST RACK OF
SPRING LAMB

BABY CARROTS GLAZED WITH
BALSAMIC BUTTER

GRATIN POTATOES

VEGETARIAN ALTERNATIVE:
MUSHROOM AND CHEESE
GOUGÈRE

TURKISH DELIGHT
PANNA COTTA

### SUNDAY TEA
SCONES

HOME-MADE CLOTTED
CREAM

# Friday Night Supper

## soup au pistou with parmesan

4 medium-sized potatoes, peeled and very finely diced

3–4 tomatoes, peeled and chopped

200g vermicelli

500g French beans, cut into 2cm pieces

salt and pepper

150g Parmesan cheese, finely grated

mild olive oil

PISTOU:

6 fat garlic cloves, peeled

large bunch of basil

1 large bunch of parsley

1 large tomato, grilled and skin and seeds removed

1 Bring 1.5 litres of water (or stock, if you prefer) up to the boil in a saucepan and add some salt. Add the potatoes and 3–4 chopped tomatoes to the water and cook until the potatoes are tender (about 10–15 minutes). Add the vermicelli and beans and continue to cook for 5–6 minutes until they are tender. Taste for seasoning and add pepper.

2 While the vegetables are cooking, make the pistou by blitzing the garlic, basil, parsley and tomato in a food processor to form a thick paste. Stir 3 tablespoons of the vegetable broth into the paste.

3 When the soup is ready, pour it into a large, warm tureen. Stir in the herb paste, scatter over the grated Parmesan cheese and drizzle in some olive oil. Serve with salami bread (see below).

Aga cooking: Cook the soup on the Simmering or Boiling Plate.

## salami bread

1 tbsp torn basil

1 tbsp chopped chives

juice of half a lemon

3 tbsp sunflower oil

salt and pepper

1 French baguette

200g salami, sliced

300g ball of mozzarella cheese, sliced

1 Whisk together the basil, chives, lemon juice, sunflower oil, salt and pepper to make a dressing.

2 Split open the bread and remove some of the dough in the middle. Spread the dressing over the bread and then layer the salami and cheese along the bottom half, repeating until all the ingredients are used up. Put the top half of the bread on, then wrap the loaf very tightly in clingfilm and press it down with tins or other heavy objects. Refrigerate overnight.

3 When you are ready to serve, remove the clingfilm and re-wrap in foil. Pre-heat the oven to 180°C/350°F/gas 4.

4 Bake for about 10 minutes or until the cheese starts to ooze. Serve straight away.

Aga cooking: Cook on the fourth set of runners in the Roasting Oven for about 10 minutes or until the cheese starts to ooze.

*soup au pistou with parmesan and salami bread*

# pistachio and almond cake

125g pistachios, shelled
100g blanched almonds
225g unsalted butter, softened
250g golden caster sugar
4 eggs
60g plain flour
1 tsp vanilla extract
zest of 1 organic lemon

TOPPING:
juice and zest of 1 lemon
50g golden caster sugar
80g pistachios, chopped

1 Grind the pistachios and almonds together in a food processor. Set aside.

2 Line a 20-cm loose-bottomed cake tin with Bake-O-Glide. Pre-heat the oven to 170°C/340°F/gas 3½.

3 Beat the butter and sugar together until light and fluffy – this is best done with an electric mixer. Beat in the eggs one at a time, alternating with the flour. Add the vanilla extract and lemon zest and fold in the nuts. Pour the mixture into the prepared tin.

4 Bake for 45–60 minutes. When the cake is cooked, the edges should pull away slightly from the sides and the top of the cake should spring back when lightly pressed in the middle. Cool the cake in the tin.

5 While the cake is cooling, make the topping. Put the juice of the lemon and sugar into a small saucepan and bring to the boil. Reduce until it is syrupy, then stir in the pistachios and lemon zest. Cool for a minute.

6 Turn the cake out onto a plate, then pour over the topping and leave to cool completely before serving.

**Aga cooking:** Slide the cold plain shelf onto the fourth set of runners in the Roasting Oven and place the tin on it. Bake for 10 minutes. Remove the cold plain shelf with the cake tin on it and slide into the Simmering Oven or, for 4-oven Aga cookers, the Baking Oven. Continue to bake for 35–60 minutes or until a skewer inserted in the centre comes out clean. Cool the cake in the tin.

# Saturday Breakfast

## full english breakfast

**PER PERSON:**

**2 eggs**

**2 rashers of bacon (back or streaky)**

**1 sausage**

**½ tomato**

**1 field mushroom**

**½ slice fried bread**

*see next page for the Aga method*

**1** Cook the sausages first. Pre-heat the oven to 180ºC/350ºF/gas 4. I recommend using Bake-O-Glide as it stop foods from sticking and makes washing up easier. Line a shallow baking tray with Bake-O-Glide and place the sausages in the tray. Do not prick them. Drizzle over a little sunflower oil, put them into the pre-heated oven and cook for 15–20 minutes, or until browned and cooked in the middle, turning them halfway through cooking. When they are ready, keep warm in a warmed ovenproof dish. You can also cook them on the hob in a pre-heated frying pan with some oil in it. In this case, invest in a splashguard – a wire mesh cover that prevents the fat from spitting over you.

**2** While the sausages are cooking, cut the tomatoes in half and put them into an ovenproof dish with the mushrooms. Drizzle over some more oil. Season with salt and pepper and slide them into the oven as well – they will take about 15 minutes. If the tomatoes are small, watch them so that they don't collapse in a heap. Keep warm when they are done.

**3** If using a frying pan for the sausages, you may also like to use it for cooking the bacon rather than grilling it. Drain off any hot fat and wipe out the inside of the pan with kitchen paper. Add some clean sunflower oil. Heat up over a medium heat and fry the bacon until crispy or however you like to serve it. Remove it and drain on kitchen paper, then turn up the heat and fry the bread – the fat does need to be hot for this. Remove and drain next to the bacon. Keep warm.

**4** When you are ready to cook the eggs, assemble the bacon, sausage, tomato, mushrooms and fried bread on a plate and keep warm. Eggs must be fried in clean fat. Heat up about 150ml of clean sunflower oil in a large, wide, seasoned frying pan. It is essential to use fresh eggs when frying otherwise the whites will spread around the pan and they will be hard to serve. Eggs must also go into hot fat or they will be absorb too much fat and be greasy.

**5** If you are confident that your eggs are fresh, crack them straight into the hot fat; if not, crack them onto a saucer and slide them into the pan. Do not overcrowd the pan and add too many eggs – two at a time is best. Baste the eggs with some of the hot fat to seal the top. When ready, remove them with a large fish slice, drain the bottom on kitchen paper and place on the plate. Serve straight away.

**6** Serve with toast, tea and coffee. Some people put out a toaster for guests to help themselves – this is up to you, but please serve toast in racks, not baskets where it goes soggy.

**Aga cooking**

**1** Use either the half-size Aga roasting tin or the full-size one, depending on how many people you are cooking for. Line it with Bake-O-Glide, and put the mushrooms and tomato halves, cut side up, on the bottom of the tin. Drizzle over a little oil and season with salt and pepper. Place the grill rack on top and put the sausages on the rack over the mushrooms and tomatoes (do not prick the sausages). Slide the tin onto the first set of runners in the Roasting Oven and cook for 10 minutes, then take the tin out of the oven, turn the sausages and lay the bacon rashers on the grill rack. Pop it back into the Roasting Oven for a further 10 minutes. Depending on the thickness of the bacon and the size of the sausages, you may need to adjust the timings accordingly.

**2** When everything is cooked, take the tin out of the oven and put the bacon, sausages, tomatoes and mushrooms on a warmed platter, cover with foil and transfer to the Simmering Oven to keep warm while you cook the eggs. If you want well-done bacon, after you transfer the sausages, tomatoes and mushrooms to the platter, take off the grill rack and put the bacon on the bottom of the tin. Place the tin onto the floor of the Roasting Oven and let the bacon cook to your liking. If you want to make fried bread, do it in exactly the same way as for well-done bacon, adding more oil if necessary. It will probably take about 5 minutes on each side.

**3 There are two ways of cooking fried eggs:** in the Aga and on the Aga.
**In the Aga:** When you remove the bacon, sausages, tomatoes and mushrooms from the tin, add a little more oil to the tin and put it onto the Roasting Oven floor to get really hot. When the oil is hot, crack the eggs into the tin one at a time. The large tin will take about 6 large eggs and the half-size tin about 3 large eggs. Baste the eggs with the fat and put the tin back into the oven for approximately 3 minutes or until they are done to your liking.

**On the Aga:** Open the Simmering Plate lid and either grease it with a little oil, or put the round pre-cut circle of Bake-O-Glide directly on the Simmering Plate surface (I always use Bake-O-Glide). Crack the egg onto the hot surface and close the lid. The egg will cook in about 2 minutes. The Simmering Plate surface can take about 3 large eggs at a time. (If you have an older Aga and the lid is dented, check to see if it touches the top of the egg when you close the lid. If it does, leave the lid open. The egg will take a little longer to cook.)

**4** To make the toast, use the Aga toasting rack (the thing that looks like a tennis racket). Open the rack, put a slice of bread in and put it onto the Boiling Plate. Close the lid but keep an eye on it as it will toast very quickly, then turn over to do the other side. To stop very fresh bread from sticking to the toaster, heat the rack up first on the Boiling Plate before putting in the toast. If you like crispy toast, leave the Boiling Plate lid open.

## orange muffins

**145g plain flour**

**75g wholewheat flour**

**130g golden caster sugar**

**2 tsp baking powder**

**110ml sour cream**

**2 large eggs, beaten**

**60ml sunflower oil**

**2 tsp vanilla extract**

**zest of 1 large organic orange**

**1** Line a muffin tin with muffin papers and set aside (this recipe makes either 6 large muffins or 12 mini muffins). Pre-heat the oven to 190ºC/375ºF/gas 5.
**2** Mix all the dry ingredients together in a large bowl and all the wet in another bowl. Make a well in the dry ingredients, add the zest and pour in the wet ingredients. Using a large rubber spatula, fold the mix together using as few strokes as possible. Spoon the mix into the muffin tin.
**3** Bake for 20 minutes or until golden. To test if they are cooked in the middle, insert the point of a knife or a skewer. If it comes out clean, they are ready. If the mix is still loose, put them back in for a few more minutes. Remove from the tin and cool on a wire rack.

**Aga cooking:** Put the tin on the grid shelf on the floor of the Roasting Oven. Slide the cold plain shelf onto the third set of runners and bake for 20–25 minutes or until golden.

## Saturday Lunch

### crab cakes with crème fraîche tartare sauce

150ml thick mayonnaise (home-made is best – see page 121)

60ml sour cream

1 tbsp Dijon mustard

2 eggs, beaten

salt and white pepper

200g dry breadcrumbs, or more if the mix is too wet

1kg white crab meat, well drained

flavourless oil

wedges of lemon, to serve

**1** Stir together the mayonnaise, sour cream, mustard, eggs and season lightly – this will depend on the quality of the mayonnaise. Gently fold in the breadcrumbs and crab meat and shape into 12 cakes, each 2.5cm thick. (You can prepare them up to this point 24 hours in advance.)

**2** Line a shallow baking tray with Bake-O-Glide and lightly brush with flavourless oil. Pre-heat the oven to 180°C/350°F/gas 4.

**3** Place the crab cakes on the tray and bake them for 8–10 minutes, then flip them over and continue to bake for another 8–10 minutes or until golden.

**4** Remove them from the oven and leave to stand for a few minutes. Serve with a wedge of lemon, a green salad and the tartare sauce (see below).

**Aga cooking:** Slide the tray into the Roasting Oven and heat it up for a few minutes. Place the crab cakes on the tray and slide onto the Roasting Oven floor. Cook them for 5–8 minutes on each side or until golden.

### crème fraîche tartare sauce

250ml mayonnaise (see page 121)

125ml crème fraîche

2–3 spring onions or a wedge of red onion, peeled

5 cornichons (tiny gherkins)

6 green olives, pitted

1 tbsp fresh tarragon leaves

1 anchovy

tarragon vinegar or lemon juice, to taste

salt and pepper

**1** Simply whiz everything up in a food processor, but not too finely as the sauce needs to have a bit of texture.

**2** Pour into a serving bowl.

*crab cakes with crème fraîche tartare sauce*

## spiced grapes

**500g ripe seedless red grapes**
**165g golden caster sugar**
**235ml white wine vinegar**
**235ml white wine**
**3 whole cloves**
**1 cinnamon stick**
**8 coriander seeds**
**2cm piece of ginger**
**½ a nutmeg, freshly grated**
**3 cardamom pods**

**1** These must be made 2 weeks in advance. Wash and dry the grapes, discarding any bruised, damaged or mouldy ones. Cut them into small clusters. Put the clusters into large, wide, sterilised bottling jars.

**2** Put the sugar, vinegar, white wine and spices into a saucepan and simmer for 2 minutes. Leave to cool to room temperature.

**3** Pour the cooled liquid over the grapes and seal. Store the jars in the fridge for a minimum of 2 weeks before using them. They will keep for up to 6 months if refrigerated.

**4** Serve a cluster of drained spiced grapes with good Cheddar cheese and with finely sliced fennel and a drizzle of honey.

**Aga cooking:** Heat the marinade on the Simmering Plate.

# Saturday Night Dinner Party

## asparagus with blood orange hollandaise

**24 thick asparagus spears**
**blood orange hollandaise (see page 60)**

**1** Prepare the asparagus for cooking either in the morning or the day before. First, sort out the asparagus: take each spear and hold it between your hands and bend it – the spear will snap at the natural woody point so there is no guesswork involved when trimming it. Tidy the ends up with a knife if necessary. Wrap the spears in damp kitchen paper, place in a plastic bag and store in the fridge.

**2** Bring the asparagus to room temperature.

**3** Bring a large shallow pan of water up to the boil. Cook the asparagus spears in boiling water for 3–5 minutes or until they are tender, but don't over-cook them.

**4** Drain and serve with the Blood Orange Hollandaise (see page 60).

**Aga cooking:** Cook the asparagus on the Boiling Plate.

*asparagus with blood orange hollandaise*

# blood orange hollandaise

3 egg yolks

1 tbsp white wine vinegar

1 tsp caster sugar

salt and pepper

175g unsalted butter, softened and cut into cubes

juice and zest of 1 large blood orange

**1** Place the egg yolks, vinegar, 1 tbsp water, sugar, salt and pepper in a bowl over a pan of simmering water (do not let the bowl come into contact with the water) and whisk until the mix leaves a ribbon trail.

**2** Whisking constantly, drop in the cubes of butter one at a time – don't be tempted to drop in the next cube until the previous one has been absorbed. This will take some time. When all the butter is mixed in, you will have a thick velvety sauce.

**3** Place the orange juice and zest in a small saucepan over a gentle heat. Reduce by half and add this to the sauce and serve poured over the asparagus (see page 58). Make this sauce no more than 20 minutes before you wish to serve it.

**Aga cooking:** Cook on the Simmering Plate.

# herbed roast rack of spring lamb

3 shallots, peeled

3–4 ransoms (wild garlic), washed and trimmed, or 2–3 cloves of garlic, peeled

2 tbsp fresh rosemary

2 tbsp fresh parsley

50g butter

salt and pepper

6 tbsp fresh breadcrumbs

4 racks of spring lamb, French trimmed, allowing 3–4 ribs per person, skin removed and fat removed

**1** Pre-heat the oven to 200ºC/400ºF/gas 6.

**2** Put the shallots, ransoms or garlic, herbs, butter, salt and pepper into the bowl of a food processor. Whiz until it is all thoroughly chopped and combined. Remove the blade and mix in the breadcrumbs.

**3** Put a shallow roasting tin in the oven to heat up. Place the lamb in the roasting tin and cook for 10 minutes. Remove from the oven, press the herb mixture onto the lamb meat and continue cooking for a further 10–15 minutes, or until it is cooked to your liking.

**Aga cooking:** Put a shallow roasting tin into the Roasting Oven to heat up. Remove the tin from the oven, place the lamb in the tin and slide onto the third set of runners in the Roasting Oven. Cook for 10 minutes, then press the herb mixture onto the lamb and continue cooking as above.

## baby carrots glazed with balsamic butter

**60g unsalted butter, at room temperature**

**2–3 tbsp aged balsamic vinegar**

**salt**

**3 ransom leaves (wild garlic), chopped**

**pinch of sugar**

**900g baby spring carrots, with a little bit of green top**

**1** Beat the butter, balsamic vinegar, salt, ransom leaves and sugar together until combined.

**2** Put the carrots into a saucepan and add about 150ml water and the balsamic butter. Cut a circle of greaseproof paper and make a hole in the centre. Put the circle over the carrots and press down.

**3** Bring the pan up to the boil, then turn it down and simmer for 10–15 minutes. I like my carrots crunchy but you can cook them for however long it takes to get them the way you prefer them.

**Aga cooking:** Use the Boiling and Simmering Plates and cook as above, or cook in the Simmering Oven.

## gratin potatoes

**60g butter, plus more for greasing gratin dish**

**1kg potatoes, peeled and thinly sliced**

**½ tsp fresh thyme**

**1 clove of garlic, peeled and thinly sliced**

**salt and pepper**

**2–3 anchovies, mashed (optional)**

**250ml double cream**

**1** Pre-heat the oven to 180ºC/350ºF/gas 4.

**2** Brush a gratin dish with some melted butter. Layer the potatoes, thyme, garlic, salt and pepper in the dish until all the ingredients are used up, finishing with some thyme and seasoning on the top. If using anchovies, add them to the layers. Pour over the cream. Dot the butter on top.

**3** Cook for 50–60 minutes, or until the potatoes are tender and the top is nicely browned.

**Aga cooking:** Cook the gratin on the second or third set of runners in the Roasting Oven for 40–45 minutes, or until the potatoes are tender and the top is nicely browned.

# mushroom and cheese gougère vegetarian main course alternative

**FILLING:**

15g butter

1 tbsp sunflower oil

1 small onion, peeled and finely chopped

250g mushrooms, sliced

1 tbsp chopped flat leaf parsley

**CHEESE SAUCE:**

20g butter

20g plain flour

300ml warm milk

salt and pepper

150g Gruyère cheese, finely grated

1 tsp Dijon mustard

**GOUGÈRE:**

75g butter, cut into pieces

100g strong plain flour, sifted onto a sheet of greaseproof paper, seasoned with salt and pepper

3 eggs, beaten in a measuring jug

75g Gruyère cheese, grated, plus a little extra for topping

**1** Grease a 23-cm oval shallow ovenproof dish with butter. Place the dish on a baking tray.

**2** To make the filling, heat up the butter and oil in a frying pan, add the onions and mushrooms and fry until they are soft and tender. Drain on a piece of kitchen paper.

**3** To make the cheese sauce, melt the butter in a small saucepan over a medium heat. Add the flour to the butter and stir well with a wooden spoon until it turns into a glossy paste. Gradually pour in the warm milk, a little at a time, stirring or whisking all the time until all of the milk is incorporated and you have a smooth sauce. Simmer the sauce for 3–5 minutes, whisking occasionally, so that the flour is cooked. Do not let the sauce burn or catch on the bottom. Remove from the heat and stir in the cheese and mustard. Taste for seasoning. Cover the surface of the sauce with clingfilm so that a skin doesn't form.

**4** Mix the onions and mushrooms and the parsley into the cheese sauce. (You can make the filling to this stage ahead of time if you wish.)

**5** To make the gougère paste, put 200ml cold water and the butter into a saucepan. Bring it to the boil. Remove it from the heat, quickly add in the flour and stir vigorously with a wooden spoon until well combined and the mixture comes away from the sides of the pan – this will take a minute or so. (The mixture goes through a stage of looking terrible but keep beating until it turns glossy.) Cool for 5–10 minutes.

**6** Beat in the eggs a little at a time until it is a thick and glossy paste (you may not need to use all the beaten egg). Stir in the cheese.

**7** Pre-heat the oven to 180°C/350°F/gas 4.

**8** Drop heaped tablespoons of the gougère paste around the sides of the prepared dish. Spoon the filling into the centre and scatter the extra cheese on top.

**9** Bake for 25–30 minutes or until it has risen and is golden brown. Serve straight away.

**Aga cooking:** Make the filling on the Simmering Plate. Cook the cheese sauce on the Simmering Plate. Bring the water and butter for the gougère paste to the boil on the Boiling Plate. When assembled, slide the dish onto the fourth set of runners in the Roasting Oven and bake for 10–15 minutes. Slide in the cold plain shelf just above (give it room to rise) and continue to cook for another 30–35 minutes or until it has risen and is golden brown.

## turkish delight panna cotta

**1.2 litres double cream**

**4cm strip of organic orange (peel it with a potato peeler, leaving the white pith behind)**

**3 gelatine leaves**

**150ml milk**

**few drops of organic pink food colouring (optional)**

**4 tbsp rosewater**

**100g icing sugar**

**8–10 squares of rose Turkish Delight, chopped into smaller squares and dusted in more icing sugar**

**organic edible rose petals**

**1** Pour 900ml of the cream into a pan, add the orange peel. Bring to the boil, then turn the heat down and simmer until it is reduced to a third. Remove the orange peel and set aside.

**2** Soak the gelatine leaves in the milk until soft. Remove the gelatine and set aside.

**3** Heat the milk in a saucepan until boiling, then remove from heat, add the gelatine back in and stir until it has dissolved.

**4** Pour the hot milk into the hot cream, stir and sieve into a bowl. Leave to cool completely.

**5** When it is cold, stir in a few drops of the pink food colouring and the rosewater. Whip the remaining cream with the icing sugar and fold it into the cooled cream-milk mixture. Pour into six bowls. Cover and allow to set in the fridge. To serve, turn out onto plates and serve with a few pieces of the Turkish Delight and a rose petal.

**Aga cooking:** Cook the cream and orange peel on the Simmering Plate. Heat the milk on the Boiling Plate.

# Sunday Breakfast

## scrambled eggs

**12 eggs**
**salt**
**250ml whipping cream**
**75g unsalted butter**
**bread, for toasting**

**1** Crack the eggs into a glass bowl. Add a little salt and the cream and beat the eggs gently.

**2** Melt half the butter in a large non-stick pan. Pour in the eggs. Stir the eggs constantly with a wooden fork or spoon until they just start to form soft curds. Remove from the heat and add the rest of the butter. Stir in, making sure it is still wet and soft.

**3** While the eggs are cooking, toast the bread (or ask someone else to do this). Serve straight away with thin slices of Maple-glazed Ham (see page 64). You may want to pass around more maple syrup to drizzle over the ham.

**Aga cooking:** Cook the eggs as above on the Simmering Plate.

# maple-glazed ham

Cooking a whole ham on the bone does take a bit of time but nothing tastes better than your own glazed ham, and it will keep for ages and feed a lot of people. The best way to keep a ham is to wrap it in a damp piece of muslin. Ham is great to have on hand when you have people to stay as you can serve it for lunch or use it in sandwiches.

A 5.5–6kg ham will feed about 20 people; a 6.5–7.5kg ham will feed about 30 people. I suggest buying an organic ham on the bone as, in my opinion, they have the best flavour. The ham has to be soaked in cold water – do ask your supplier what they recommend, as the soaking time will depend on how much salt is used in the curing process. I usually use a plastic bucket or washing-up bowl – it depends on how big the ham is. I also like to change the water halfway through the soaking time.

There are two options for cooking the ham: boil and bake or bake only. The choice is yours.

**boil and bake method**

**Boiling method:**

**1** Remove the ham from the soaking water and put it in a pot large enough to hold the ham. Cover the ham with fresh cold water and bring to the boil. Turn the heat down to a gentle simmer and simmer for about 5 hours for a 5.5–6kg joint or 6–6½ hours for a 6.5–7.5kg joint. It is done when the juices run clear when a skewer is put through the thickest part.

**2** Remove the ham from the water, peel off the skin and score the fat. Put the ham into a large roasting tin. Mix 300ml maple syrup with 3–4 tablespoons soft muscovado sugar. Press the mix into the fat, using it all up.

**3** Pre-heat the oven to 200ºC/400ºF/gas 6. Bake the ham for 20–30 minutes or until it is nicely coloured and glazed. Eat the ham hot or cold.

**Aga boiling method:**

**1** Remove the ham from the soaking water and put it in a pot large enough to hold the ham. Cover the ham with fresh cold water. Bring to the boil on the Boiling Plate, transfer it to the Simmering Plate and simmer for 20–30 minutes, then transfer it to the Simmering Oven for about 5 hours for a 5.5–6kg joint (6–6½ hours for a 6.5–7.5kg joint). It is done when the juices run clear when a skewer is put through the thickest part.

**2** Remove it from the water and peel off the skin and score the fat. Put the ham into the large roasting tin. Mix 300ml maple syrup with 3–4 tablespoons soft muscovado sugar. Press the mix into the fat, using it all up.

**3** Hang the tin on the third set of runners in the Roasting Oven and bake the ham for 20–30 minutes or until it is nicely coloured and glazed. Eat the ham hot or cold.

**baking method**

**1** Pre-heat the oven to 180°C/350°F/gas 4.

**2** Remove the ham from the soaking water and drain. Lay two long pieces of foil in a large roasting tin, one lengthways, one widthways, to form a cross. You need enough foil for the ham to sit in a tent of foil. Bring the foil up around the ham, leaving enough room for air to circulate around the joint.

**3** Cook the ham for 20 minutes per 450g. The ham is done when the juices run clear when a skewer is inserted in the thickest part of the ham.

**4** Remove the joint from the oven and turn the temperature up to 200°C/400°F/gas 6.

**5** Pull back the foil and remove the skin – it will be very hot so protect your hands. Score the fat. Mix 300ml maple syrup with 3–4 tablespoons soft muscovado sugar. Press the mix into the fat, using it all up. Eat the ham hot or cold.

**6** Cook for 20 minutes or until it is nicely coloured and glazed.

**Aga cooking:** Hang the tin on the fourth set of runners in the Roasting Oven and bake for 18 minutes per 450g. For 4-oven Aga cookers, bake for 20 minutes per 450g in the Baking Oven. Remove the foil and continue as above with the glaze. After adding the maple glaze, cook for 20 minutes in the Roasting Oven.

# Sunday Lunch

## citrus-baked chicken with artichoke hearts

olive oil

2 medium onions, peeled and cut into wedges

6 baby artichoke hearts, cut in half (if you can't find fresh, use tinned and drain them)

6 organic chicken breasts, skin on

a glass of fruity white wine

salt and pepper

375ml chicken stock

zest of a lime and a lemon

8–10 cherry tomatoes

50g stoned black Kalamata olives, halved

1 Pre-heat the oven to 180°C/350°F/gas 4.

2 Heat up a large ovenproof frying pan and add 1 tablespoon olive oil. Add the onion wedges. Gently char and soften them, then remove them to a plate. Add the artichoke hearts to the pan, soften them, add to the plate of onions.

3 Brown the chicken breasts in the same pan, a few at a time.

4 Pour in the white wine, scrape up all the bits left on the bottom of the pan and cook for a few minutes until it has almost all evaporated.

5 Put the chicken breasts back into the pan, then add the onions and artichokes. Season with salt and pepper. Pour in the stock and half of the zest. Bring to the boil, then transfer to the oven for 15 minutes. Remove the pan from the oven and add the tomatoes, olives and the remaining zest. Return to the oven and cook for a further 8–10 minutes or until the breasts are cooked.

6 Remove the breasts to a warmed plate and bubble up the sauce over a high heat for a few minutes to reduce the sauce, then pour over the chicken and serve. This can be served hot or cold.

**Aga cooking:** Cook the onions and artichokes as above on the Roasting Oven floor or on the Boiling Plate. Brown the chicken on the Roasting Oven floor or on the Boiling Plate, then cook the entire dish in the Roasting Oven for 10 minutes. Reduce the sauce on the Boiling Plate.

## gratin of spring vegetables

500g baby carrots, trimmed but with a bit of the green stalk left on

80g butter, plus more for greasing gratin dish

500g potatoes, peeled and thinly sliced

500g baby leeks

½ tsp freshly chopped thyme

finely grated zest of an unwaxed lemon

salt and pepper

375ml whole milk

1 Pre-heat the oven to 180°C/350°F/gas 4.

2 Bring a pan of water to the boil, add the carrots and blanch for 1–2 minutes. Drain.

3 Brush a gratin dish with melted butter, then layer the potatoes, carrots, leeks, herbs, lemon zest, salt and pepper in the dish until all the ingredients are used up, finishing with some of the herbs, lemon zest and seasoning on the top. Pour over the milk.

4 Cook for 40 minutes or until the vegetables are tender and the top is nicely browned. This can be cooked beforehand and reheated if you wish.

**Aga cooking:** Blanch the carrots on the Boiling Plate, then cook in the Roasting Oven for 20–30 minutes.

*citrus-baked chicken with artichoke hearts*

# custard tart

**SWEET PASTRY:**

**340g plain flour**

**225g butter, cold and cubed**

**1 egg, from the fridge**

**30g caster sugar**

**FILLING:**

**3 egg whites**

**5 egg yolks**

**575ml double cream**

**1 whole vanilla pod**

**50g golden caster sugar**

**20g unsalted butter, softened**

**nutmeg**

**1** To make the pastry, put all the ingredients into a food processor and pulse until the mixture comes together to form a ball. Add a drop of cold water if the mixture is too crumbly. Wrap in clingfilm and rest in the fridge for at least 30 minutes.

**2** Bring the pastry to room temperature. Roll it out to line a deep, 22-cm tart tin. Line the pastry with greaseproof paper and fill with baking beans.

**3** Pre-heat the oven to 180°C/350°F/gas 4. Blind-bake the pastry case for 10 minutes. Set aside. Turn the oven down to 160°C/325°F/gas 3.

**4** In a bowl, whisk together the egg whites and yolks, then set aside.

**5** Pour the cream into a saucepan, scrape the vanilla pod seeds into the milk and add the sugar. Gently bring to a simmer. Take the cream off the heat and add to the whisked eggs, little by little, whisking constantly until it is all combined. Grate about half a nutmeg into the custard, then pour the custard into the pastry case. Grate over more nutmeg.

**6** Bake for 35-45 minutes. The filling should still have a bit of a wobble when it comes out. Leave to cool completely.

**Aga cooking:** There is no need to blind-bake the pastry case. Heat the cream on the Simmering Plate. To bake the tart, put the tin on the Roasting Oven floor. Slide the cold plain shelf onto the runners just above and bake for 35–45 minutes or until the top is golden brown but still has a bit of a wobble. Check the tart after 20 minutes and turn it if one side is browning more than the other. You may need to remove the plain shelf and slide in another cold one as they are only good for 30 minutes or so, depending how hot your oven is when starting out. If you wish, after 20 minutes, you can move the tart to the Simmering Oven for a further 30 minutes.

# Sunday Tea

## scones

**225g self-raising flour**
**1½ tbsp caster sugar**
**pinch of salt**
**40g butter, softened**
**150ml milk**
**beaten egg, to glaze**

**1** Pre-heat the oven to 190°/375°F/gas 5. Line a baking tray with Bake-O-Glide.

**2** Combine the flour, sugar and salt in the bowl of an electric mixer with the paddle hook. Add the butter in pieces, then add the milk. Mix until the dough just starts to hold together.

**3** Turn out onto a floured surface. Roll the dough to a thickness of 2cm and cut out the scones with a fluted cutter. Put them on the prepared baking trays and brush with a beaten egg glaze. Sprinkle over a little more sugar if you wish.

**4** Bake for 8–10 minutes or until golden. Remove from the oven and cool on a wire rack. Serve with strawberry jam and clotted cream (see below). This quantity will make 8–10 scones.

**Aga cooking:** Slide the baking tray onto the third set of runners in the Roasting Oven and bake for 8–10 minutes or until golden.

## home-made clotted cream

**750ml double cream, preferably Jersey**
**25g butter**

**1** Mix the cream and the butter in a heavy-based saucepan. Put it onto the lowest heat and slowly turn up the heat and bring up to a rapid simmer. Do not let it boil over. Stir it constantly with a wooden spoon so that bubbles are breaking the surface but it is not sticking at the bottom. Reduce to half – this takes 8–10 minutes.

**2** When it is ready, pour it into a shallow, flat dish and allow to cool, then refrigerate until ready to serve.

**Aga cooking:** Cook as above on the Simmering Plate.

# Summer House Party serves 6

### SATURDAY BREAKFAST
STUFFED 'FRENCH' TOAST
BAKERY BASKET

### SATURDAY LUNCH
PEPPER AND TOMATO SUMMER PUDDING
SOUR CREAM AND DILL CUCUMBER
OOZING BRIE

### SATURDAY NIGHT DINNER PARTY
CRUSHED BROAD BEAN AND MINT BRUSCHETTA WITH CHORIZO SAUSAGES
LANGOUSTINES WITH ROASTED TOMATO CREAM SAUCE
VEGETARIAN ALTERNATIVE: EGGPLANT PARMIGIANO
LEMON VERBENA STRAWBERRIES AND RASPBERRIES WITH MERINGUES

### SUNDAY BREAKFAST
POACHED EGGS ON MUFFINS WITH MARMITE BUTTER
BAKERY BASKET

### SUNDAY LUNCH
POACHED SALMON WITH HERB HOLLANDAISE
NEW POTATOES
GREEN AND YELLOW WAXED BEANS
NECTARINE AND LEMON CREAM TART

### SUNDAY TEA
STRAWBERRY SANDWICHES
FRESH HERB TISANES

### FRIDAY NIGHT SUPPER
PRAWN, MANGO AND CASHEW SALAD
BLUEBERRY PIE

## Friday Night Supper

### prawn, mango and cashew salad

**200g thick Greek yoghurt**

**4 tbsp mayonnaise (see page 121)**

**juice and zest of 1 lime or a little more to taste (or use juice of a lemon and half the zest)**

**1 tbsp mango chutney**

**1 tbsp garam masala**

**salt**

**800g cooked tiger prawns, peeled, deveined and cut in half horizontally so they still look like prawns**

**1 tbsp freshly snipped chives**

**1 large ripe mango, peeled and diced**

**80g chopped cashew nuts, plus some whole cashews to garnish**

1 Mix the yoghurt, mayonnaise, juice and zest, chutney, and garam masala together, then season with salt. (I like to heat the garam masala for a few minutes in a frying pan first, to take the raw edge off it.)

2 Fold in the prawns, chives, mango and chopped cashews. Garnish with a handful of whole cashews and serve with a rocket salad.

*prawn, mango and cashew salad*

# blueberry pie

**SWEET SHORTCRUST PASTRY:**

720g plain flour

240g caster sugar

pinch of salt

360g unsalted butter, cold and cubed

3 eggs, beaten

**FILLING:**

65g flour

60g unsalted butter, cold and cubed

1kg blueberries

60g caster sugar

1 beaten egg yolk, for egg wash

**1** To make the pastry, sift the flour, sugar and salt into the food processor, then add the butter and process for 30 seconds. Add the eggs and process again until it forms a ball (you may have to add a little cold water, 1 tablespoon at a time, if the mixture is dry). Stop immediately, wrap the pastry in clingfilm and rest in the fridge for a minimum of 30 minutes.

**2** Pre-heat the oven to 170°C/340°F/gas 3½.

**3** Line a 27-cm pie dish with the pastry. Line the pastry with greaseproof paper, fill with baking beans and blind-bake the pastry for 10-12 minutes. Set aside.

**4** To make the filling, put the flour and butter into the food processor and pulse until it is crumbly. Transfer it to a bowl and add the blueberries. Tip the mixture into the pastry case.

**5** Pre-heat the oven to 170°C/340°F/gas 3½.

**6** Roll out the remaining pastry and, using a leaf-shaped cookie cutter, cut out lots of leaves and arrange them decoratively on top of the blueberries, almost completely covering the pie. (You will have extra pastry left over so freeze it for another day.) Brush the top of the pie with the egg wash. Bake for 35–40 minutes or until it is golden.

**Aga cooking:** There is no need to blind-bake the pastry case. Bake the pie on the Roasting Oven floor with the cold plain shelf on the fourth set of runners for 30–35 minutes or until the crust is golden.

# Saturday Breakfast

## stuffed 'french' toast

2 oranges

4 eggs

50ml double cream

6 slices of bread, at least 3cm thick

unsalted butter

marmalade

icing sugar

**1** To segment the oranges, use a very sharp knife. Cut the peel and pith away from the flesh. Hold the orange over a bowl to catch the juices and carefully dissect out each segment, leaving behind the membrane and skin. Repeat all the way round the orange, squeezing out any juice from the pithy remains. Set the segments aside, leaving them in their juices. This can be done a day in advance.

**2** In a large flat dish, combine the eggs and cream and beat well. Dip the bread into the eggy mix on both sides.

**3** Heat up some butter in a large frying pan until frothing. Put the eggy bread into the pan and cook for a few minutes, then flip it over and continue cooking until both sides are golden.

**4** Cut a pocket into the side of each slice of bread. Spread a little marmalade in the pocket and stuff with some orange segments. Transfer to a warm plate, spread more butter on the bread and dust with icing sugar. Serve for breakfast, with streaky bacon to accompany if you wish.

**Aga cooking:** Cook the eggy bread directly on the Simmering Plate on a piece of Bake-O-Glide.

# Saturday Lunch

## pepper and tomato summer pudding

There are no real measurements here as it depends on the size of the pudding basin and your personal taste. You will need 1–1.5kg of tomatoes to feed 6 people.

loaf of stale white bread

olive oil

passata

lemon juice

Worcestershire sauce

Tabasco sauce

salt and pepper

fresh plum tomatoes, peeled and chopped or, if in a rush, unpeeled and chopped

1 jar of roasted and peeled peppers, drained of oil

cloves of garlic, peeled and crushed

balsamic vinegar

lots of fresh basil, torn

lots of fresh oregano, chopped

**1** Slice the bread, remove the crusts and put to one side. Grease a pudding basin with olive oil.

**2** Pour the passata onto a flat dish and season it with lemon juice, Worcestershire sauce, Tabasco and salt and pepper, then dip the slices of bread into it and line the pudding basin with them.

**3** Put the tomatoes and peppers into the lined basin and add salt and pepper, garlic, olive oil, balsamic vinegar, basil and oregano. Gently stir it, being careful not to tear the bread at the bottom. Taste for seasoning.

**4** Make a lid for the pudding with more passata-seasoned bread, tucking it in all around to seal in the tomato mixture. Cover the top with clingfilm and a plate, and put a can on top to weigh it down. Leave in the fridge overnight.

**5** To serve, remove the pudding from the basin onto a plate, and cut into wedges.

## sour cream and dill cucumber

1 large organic cucumber, seeds removed and very thinly sliced

2 tbsp white wine vinegar

1 tbsp sugar

½ tbsp salt

1 large bunch of dill, chopped

250ml sour cream

**1** Put the cucumbers into a bowl. Put the vinegar, sugar and salt into a jug and whisk together – you must taste to get the balance of sweet and sour to your liking. Adjust seasoning and pour over the cucumbers. Leave for a minimum of 1 hour, or longer if possible.

**2** Drain the cucumbers, reserving the liquid, and stir in the chopped dill and sour cream. Thin down with a little of the liquid, if required. Serve with the pepper and tomato summer pudding, and finish the lunch with a delicious oozing Brie.

*pepper and tomato summer pudding*

# Saturday Night Dinner Party

## crushed broad bean and mint bruschetta with chorizo sausages

**1.5kg broad beans**

**1 tbsp finely chopped mint**

**1 tbsp torn basil**

**salt and pepper**

**6 long slices of sourdough bread**

**1 clove of garlic, peeled**

**olive oil, for serving**

**50g Parmesan cheese, grated**

**200g chorizo sausage or salami, thinly sliced**

**1** To shell and pod the broad beans, have a bowl of iced water ready for blanching. Shell the beans from their tough pods. Bring a pan of water up to the boil and cook the beans in boiling water for 2–3 minutes or until they start to wrinkle and they still have a bit of bite to them. Remove the beans with a slotted spoon and plunge them into the iced water immediately. Drain from the iced water and carefully peel off the membrane. Put the bright green beans into a bowl. This can be done in advance.

**2** Reserve a handful of the beans for garnish. Crush the remaining broad beans with a fork or pestle and mortar – you want them to retain some texture. Mix in the herbs and season with salt and pepper.

**3** Toast the bread slices and rub each one with the garlic clove.

**4** Spoon the crushed beans onto the toast, drizzle over some olive oil and sprinkle over the Parmesan. Serve each one with a few slices of chorizo.

**Aga cooking:** Cook the beans on the Boiling Plate.

## langoustines with roasted tomato cream sauce

**32 langoustines**

**200g butter, at room temperature**

**salt and pepper**

**4 cloves of garlic, peeled and crushed**

**olive oil**

**1** Pre-heat the oven to 200°C/400°F/gas 6. Put a large, shallow baking tray into the oven to heat up while you prepare the langoustines.

**2** Split the langoustines in half using a sharp knife or scissors.

**3** Combine the butter, salt, pepper, garlic and a splash of olive oil together in a bowl. Spread onto the langoustine halves.

**4** Remove the baking tray from the oven, place the langoustines on the tray and slide back into the oven. Cook for 5–8 minutes, or until just cooked. You may have to do this in batches.

**5** Serve straight away with Roasted Tomato Cream Sauce (see page 78) and crusty bread.

**Aga cooking:** Heat up the baking tray in the Roasting Oven. Cook in the Roasting Oven for 5–8 minutes.

*langoustines with roasted tomato cream sauce*

# roasted tomato cream sauce

**250g vine-ripened tomatoes**

**1 large fat garlic clove, unpeeled**

**1 tbsp olive oil**

**salt and pepper**

**1 handful of fresh basil leaves, torn**

**100ml vegetable stock**

**100ml double cream**

**1** Pre-heat the oven to 180°C/350°F/gas 5.

**2** Put the tomatoes and unpeeled garlic clove into a heavy roasting tin and drizzle with the oil. Season with salt and pepper and add the torn basil leaves. Put the roasting tin in the oven and cook for about 20 minutes or until the tomatoes and garlic are soft.

**3** When the tomatoes are cooked, remove the garlic clove from the tin and squeeze the pulpy flesh from the skin into a saucepan. Pour the tomatoes into a sieve and catch the juice in the saucepan.

**4** Add the stock and cream to the juices in the saucepan. Bring the sauce to the boil. Turn the heat down to a simmer and reduce by half.

**5** Taste for seasoning. Serve with the langoustines (see page 76). This sauce can be made a day in advance.

**Aga cooking:** Place the roasting tin containing the tomatoes and garlic on the Boiling or Simmering Plate and cook as above. Reduce the sauce on the Boiling or Simmering Plate.

# eggplant parmigiano (vegetarian main course alternative)

**1.5kg aubergines, cut lengthways into slices 1–2cm thick**

**salt and pepper**

**olive oil**

**1 clove of garlic, peeled**

**500ml passata**

**2 large bunches of basil**

**50g anchovies in olive oil, chopped (optional, depending whether your vegetarian guests eat fish)**

**220g Parmesan cheese, grated**

**250g ball of Mozzarella cheese, thinly sliced**

**1** Put the aubergine slices in a bowl. Sprinkle a tablespoon of salt over them and pour enough water over to cover them. Stand for 30 minutes. Drain them well and pat the slices dry on kitchen paper.

**2** Line a large, shallow baking tray with Bake-O-Glide, brush some oil on it and rub it with the garlic clove.

**3** Pre-heat the oven to 180°C/350°F/gas 4 and heat up the tray in the oven.

**4** Lay the aubergine slices on the heated tray and brush them with more olive oil. Slide the tray into the oven and cook for about 10–12 minutes, flipping the aubergines over halfway through so that both sides brown. Alternatively, fry the aubergines in batches in a frying pan.

**5** Brush a little more olive oil into a deep ovenproof dish (about 25 x 35cm) and rub with the garlic clove. Discard the clove. Spoon over some of the passata, scatter over a few basil leaves and some anchovies (if using). Lay some of the aubergine slices on top, then a little more passata and some of the cheeses. Season the layers with salt and pepper. Continue layering until everything is used up, finishing with the cheeses. (The dish can be made to this stage, covered with clingfilm and stored in the fridge the day before. Bring to room temperature before baking.)

**6** When you are ready to bake it, pre-heat the oven to 180°C/350°F/gas 4 and bake for 20–25 minutes or until golden and crusty. Serve with a salad and lots of bread.

**Aga cooking:** Cook the aubergine slices in a frying pan on the Boiling or Simmering Plate, or in a pre-heated tin on the Roasting Oven floor for 8–10 minutes. Bake the dish on the third set of runners in the Roasting Oven for 20–25 minutes or until it is golden and crusty.

# lemon verbena strawberries and raspberries with meringues

**MERINGUES:**

**lemon half**

**4 egg whites**

**225g caster sugar**

**80g sliced almonds**

**TOPPING:**

**100g caster sugar**

**8–10 lemon verbena leaves**

**500g strawberries**

**500g raspberries**

**450ml double cream**

**1** Pre-heat the oven to 150°C/300°F/gas 2. Line a baking tray with Bake-O-Glide.

**2** Before you start to make the meringues, make sure your bowl and beaters or whisk are scrupulously clean. Rub a lemon half over the beaters and the inside of the bowl.

**3** Put the egg whites into the bowl and start to whisk them on a medium speed, increasing the speed to high as you go. First the whites will bubble and turn frothy, then they will form into soft floppy peaks and finally they will reach the stiff peak stage. Add the sugar one spoonful at a time until it is used up. Fold in 50g of the almonds.

**4** Spoon the meringue mix onto the lined baking tray. Scatter over the remaining almonds.

**5** Bake for 1½–2 hours. If you like your meringues very dry, when cooked, turn each meringue on its side, switch off the oven, put the tray back into the oven and leave to dry out for another 30–45 minutes.

**6** To make the topping, blitz the sugar with the lemon verbena in a food processor and set aside. Hull and quarter the strawberries, tip into a bowl and spoon over some of the lemon verbena sugar. Leave to macerate for an hour or so. You may not need all the sugar. Taste for sweetness.

**7** When you are ready to serve, mix the raspberries into the strawberries. Whip the cream so that it holds soft peaks. Spoon some cream onto a plate, top with a meringue, then spoon over some of the fruit with the juice. Sprinkle with any leftover sugar. (If you wish, the meringues can be made a few days ahead of time and stored in an airtight tin.)

**Aga cooking:** Cook the meringues in the Simmering Oven for 2–2½ hours.

# Sunday Breakfast

## poached eggs on muffins with marmite butter

**PER PERSON**
**Marmite**
**unsalted butter, softened**
**2 eggs**
**vinegar**
**1 muffin**

**1** First beat the Marmite into the butter – the amount of Marmite will depend on how much you like it! Do it to taste. This can be done a few days in advance and stored in the fridge.

**2** The eggs must be very fresh for successful poaching. Bring a saucepan filled half-full with water and 1 teaspoon of vinegar up to a gentle simmer over a medium heat. As soon as you see the first bubbles start to appear, crack the eggs into the pan and cook the eggs for 2–3 minutes. Remove the eggs from the water using a slotted spoon, drain on a piece of kitchen paper (or a stale crust of bread) and serve straight away.

**3** While the eggs are cooking, split the muffin in half and toast. To serve, spread each toasted muffin half with the Marmite butter and top with a poached egg.

**Aga cooking:** Poach the eggs as above on the Simmering or Boiling Plate. Toast the muffins using the Aga toasting rack on the Boiling Plate.

# Sunday Lunch

## poached salmon with herb hollandaise

1.5 kg whole salmon (allow 125–175g per person)

2–3 tbsp lemon juice or lemon slices

10–12 peppercorns

small bunch of parsley, stalks on

1 carrot, peeled and sliced

1 small onion, peeled and sliced

1 bay leaf

**1** Place the fish in the fish kettle and pour in enough cold water to cover it. (If you don't have a fish kettle, use a large roasting tin and cover with foil. If the fish is very large you can place it in a half-moon shape, pour over the liquid and cover with foil.) Add the rest of the ingredients.

**2** Bring to the boil and boil for 1 minute.

**3** Remove from the heat. To serve it hot, leave it for 15–20 minutes. (To serve it cold, leave the fish in the liquid overnight.)

**4** Remove the fish from the kettle or tin and place it on a warm plate large enough to hold it. To skin the fish, using a sharp knife, score around the head, gills and tail. Carefully peel back the skin in long strips and discard. Do one side at a time. Scrape off any brown bits without tearing the pink flesh.

**5** To serve the fish, use a thin-bladed sharp knife. Cut along the backbone and carefully slide the knife under the flesh to remove it from the bones. Lift off a portion and serve. When you have removed all the meat from the top half, discard the bones and continue serving. Serve with Herb Hollandaise (see below) and new potatoes.

**Aga cooking:** Cook the salmon as above on the Boiling Plate.

## herb hollandaise

3 egg yolks

1 tbsp lemon juice, plus more to taste

1 teaspoon caster sugar

salt and pepper

175g butter, cut into cubes and softened

100ml double cream

1 tbsp freshly chopped dill

1 tbsp freshly chopped tarragon

**1** Place the egg yolks, lemon juice, 1 tablespoon water, sugar, salt and pepper in a bowl over a pan of simmering water (do not let the bowl come into contact with the water) and whisk until the mix leaves a ribbon trail.

**2** Whisking constantly, drop in the cubes of butter one at a time to make a thick, velvety sauce – don't drop in the next cube until the previous one has been absorbed.

**3** Whip the cream until soft peaks form, then fold the cream and herbs into the sauce. Taste for seasoning and serve.

**Aga cooking:** Heat the sauce on the Simmering Plate.

*poached salmon with herb hollandaise*

## green and yellow waxed beans

500g green beans, topped
500g yellow beans, topped
knob of butter
salt

1 Bring a large pot of water to the boil and add the beans. Cook for 3 minutes or until they are done to your taste.

2 Remove the beans from the water, drain into a warmed serving bowl. Add the knob of butter and season with salt.

**Aga cooking:** Cook the beans on the Boiling Plate.

## nectarine and lemon cream tart

3–4 ripe nectarines

**SWEET SHORTCRUST PASTRY:**
720g plain flour
240g caster sugar
pinch of salt
360g unsalted butter, cold and cubed
3 eggs, beaten

**LEMON CREAM:**
2 egg yolks
50g golden caster sugar
75ml double cream
zest of ½ an organic lemon, very finely grated on a microplane grater

1 To make the pastry, sift the flour, sugar and salt into the food processor, then add the butter and process for 30 seconds. Add the eggs and process again until it forms a ball (you may have to add a little cold water, 1 tablespoon at a time, if the mixture is dry). Stop immediately, wrap the pastry in clingfilm and rest in the fridge for a minimum of 30 minutes.

2 Pre-heat the oven to 170ºC/340ºF/gas 3½.

3 Roll out the pastry thinly and line a 20-cm pie dish. (You will probably only need half the pastry, so freeze the rest for another day.) Blind-bake the pastry case for 10–15 minutes. Cool the pastry for 10 minutes.

4 To make the filling, put the egg yolks and sugar into the bowl of an electric mixer and whisk at high speed until it has doubled in size – this will take about 10 minutes. Add the double cream and lemon zest.

5 Arrange the nectarine slices on the pastry case. Pour over the filling.

6 Turn the oven down to 160ºC/325ºF/gas 3. Bake the tart for 30 minutes or until puffed up and golden.

7 Sift icing sugar over the tart and serve with vanilla ice cream.

**Aga cooking:** There is no need to blind-bake the pastry case. Place the filled tart on the floor of the Roasting Oven and cook for 25–30 minutes or until puffed up and golden. Check after 10 minutes, and use the cold plain shelf on the bottom set of runners to deflect the heat if the tart is browning too quickly.

# Sunday Tea

## strawberry sandwiches

**1 tbsp elderflower cordial or lemon verbena cordial**

**300g strawberries, hulled and sliced thinly**

**8 slices of organic white bread, very thinly sliced**

**clotted cream (see page 69)**

**golden caster sugar**

**1** Gently fold the cordial into the strawberry slices, taking care not to break them up.

**2** Spread each slice of bread with some clotted cream. Arrange the strawberries on top of the cream on four slices, sprinkle with a little golden caster sugar, then top with another slice of bread, cream side down.

**3** Press down lightly, cut off the crusts and then cut each sandwich into four fingers.

## fresh herb tisanes

**potted fresh rosemary leaves, mint leaves or chamomile flowers**

**still mineral water**

**honey**

**lemon**

**1** For the best effect, use glass teapots and make sure the herbs are in beautiful terracotta plant pots that are clean on the bottom. Arrange the pots of herbs on the table along with a pair of Japanese scissors, silver teaspoons, glass teapot and cups.

**2** Snip the leaves from the plants into the teapot (only use one type of herb per pot) and pour over freshly boiled mineral water. Leave to infuse for a few minutes, then pour into cups. Add honey or lemon to taste or leave pure.

# Autumn House Party serves 6

### SATURDAY BREAKFAST
KIPPERS

ALL-IN-ONE FRY-UP

BAKERY BASKET

### SATURDAY LUNCH
CLASSIC BEEF CASSEROLE
WITH MASHED POTATO TOPPING

APPLE AND CUSTARD PIE

VACHERIN MONT D'OR CHEESE
AND SLOE GIN

### SATURDAY NIGHT DINNER PARTY
ROASTED FIELD MUSHROOMS
WITH GOAT'S CHEESE AND
HERBS

RACK OF VEAL WITH MUSTARD
HERB CRUST

CRUSHED POTATOES

VEGETARIAN ALTERNATIVE:
LEEK AND POTATO CAKES WITH
CHEESE SAUCE

PASSIONFRUIT MERINGUE

FIG FLORENTINES

### FRIDAY NIGHT SUPPER
TRAY-BAKED PORK
CHOPS

MASHED POTATOES WITH
PANCETTA AND PINE
NUTS

HONEY-ROASTED
PARSNIPS

OAT AND FIG COOKIES
WITH ICE CREAM

### SUNDAY BREAKFAST
CODDLED EGGS AND
SOLDIERS

FRIED PUFFBALL WITH
BACON

BAKERY BASKET

### SUNDAY LUNCH
BLOODY MARY

ROAST PHEASANT WITH
SAVOURY BREADCRUMBS

ROSEMARY-INFUSED
CHESTNUTS

GAME CHIPS

BREAD SAUCE

WILD RICE AND WILD
MUSHROOM STUFFING

PLUM AND HAZELNUT
CRUMBLE

### SUNDAY TEA
TREACLE SPONGE CAKE

# Friday Night Supper

## tray-baked pork chops

6 pork chump chops

salt and pepper

sunflower oil

1 large onion, peeled and finely sliced

1–2 cooking apples, peeled, cored and chopped

4 sprigs of fresh thyme

250ml cider

**1** Pre-heat the oven to 180ºC/350ºF/gas 4. Place a roasting tin in the oven until it is very hot.

**2** While the pan is heating up, season the chops with salt and pepper. Remove the tin from the oven and pour in some sunflower oil. Put the onion into the tin and stir so it is coated with oil. Put the tin into the oven and cook for 10 minutes until soft.

**3** Put the apples on top of the onions and the chops on top of them. Tuck in the thyme. Pour over the cider. Slide the tin back into the oven and cook for 10 minutes, then turn over the chops and cook for a further 10 minutes.

**4** When the chops are cooked, take the tin out of the oven, transfer the chops to a warmed plate and rest for 5 minutes.

**5** Over a low heat, bubble up any pan juices and mash the onions and apple together; add a little more cider or stock if the sauce is too thick.

**6** Check the seasoning and serve with the onion and apple sauce.

**Aga cooking:** Pre-heat a roasting tin in the Roasting Oven until it is very hot. Cook the onion in the pre-heated tin in the Roasting Oven for 8 minutes until soft. Add the apples, chops and cider. Slide the tin back into the Roasting Oven and cook for 8–10 minutes, then turn over the chops and cook for a further 8–10 minutes. Make the sauce as above on the Simmering Plate.

# honey-roasted parsnips

**900g parsnips, peeled and quartered**

**2 tbsp sunflower oil**

**2 tbsp honey**

**sea salt**

**1** Soak the parsnips in cold water for 10 minutes. Drain them well on kitchen paper, making sure they are as dry as possible.

**2** Pre-heat the oven to 200°C/400°F/gas 6.

**3** Put the parsnips in a large bowl, pour in the oil and honey and mix them well with your hands. Tip them into a shallow baking tin. Cook the parsnips for 20–30 minutes, stirring them halfway through cooking to make sure they brown on all sides.

**4** Drain on kitchen paper, sprinkle with lots of sea salt and serve.

**Aga cooking:** Cook in the Roasting Oven for 20–30 minutes, stirring halfway through cooking to make sure they brown on all sides.


# mashed potatoes with pancetta and pine nuts

**1 head of garlic**

**olive oil**

**salt and pepper**

**2.2kg potatoes, peeled and cut into chunks**

**250g butter**

**4 tbsp crème fraîche**

**TOPPING:**

**1½ tbsp sunflower oil**

**150g pancetta cubes**

**1 large red onion, peeled and thinly sliced**

**3 tbsp pine nuts**

**1** For the topping, heat the oil in a frying pan, add the pancetta and fry until cooked and starting to crisp. Toss in the onion slices and continue cooking until the pancetta and onion are crispy and golden. Drain on kitchen paper and set aside. Wipe out the pan with kitchen paper and toast the pine nuts.

**2** Pre-heat the oven to 180°C/350°F/gas 4. Place the whole head of garlic on a piece of foil large enough to wrap it in and pour over a little olive oil. Wrap it up tightly and roast it in the oven for 20–25 minutes or until it is soft. Remove the garlic from the oven and let it cool until you are able to handle it. Squeeze out the flesh, mash it in a bowl and set aside.

**3** To make the mashed potatoes, fill a large saucepan with water, add salt and potatoes and bring up to a boil. Cook for 10–12 minutes or until soft.

**4** Drain the potatoes well. Using a potato ricer, mash the potatoes until smooth. Add the butter, garlic, salt and pepper to taste and crème fraîche and beat well. Taste for seasoning. Spoon into a warm dish and scatter over the topping. (If you wish, this dish can be prepared in advance, then assembled and reheated.)

**Aga cooking:** Cook the pancetta, onion and pine nuts as above on the Simmering Plate. Cook the garlic in the Roasting Oven for 15 minutes. Cook the potatoes on the Boiling Plate for 3 minutes, then drain the water and transfer to the Simmering Oven for 20–25 minutes. Continue as above to make the mash.

*tray-baked pork chops*

# oat and fig cookies with ice cream

240g unsalted butter

450g brown sugar

pinch of salt

½ tsp ground cinnamon

1 tsp baking soda

365g self-raising flour

2 eggs

1 tsp vanilla extract

160g oatmeal

125g dried figs, finely chopped

good-quality vanilla ice cream

1 Pre-heat the oven to 180ºC/350ºF/gas 4.

2 Cream the butter and sugar together in an electric mixer using the paddle attachment.

3 Add the salt, cinnamon and baking soda to the flour.

4 Break one egg at a time into the creamed butter and sugar and mix. Stir in the vanilla extract, then add the flour until it is all incorporated. Mix in the oatmeal and chopped figs so they are evenly distributed. Drop spoonfuls of the mix 4cm apart on a baking tray. (This recipe makes about 36 cookies, depending on the size of spoon you use.)

5 Bake for 5–8 minutes or until golden. Don't over-cook them.

6 Cool on a wire rack. Sandwich the cookies together with ice cream and serve immediately. (The cookies can be baked 2–3 days in advance, if you wish, and stored in an airtight container.)

Aga cooking: Bake on the fourth set of runners in the Roasting Oven for 5–8 minutes.

# Saturday Breakfast

## kippers

Put the kippers on a shallow baking tray lined with Bake-O-Glide, splash on a bit of water and a knob of butter, and cook them under a really hot grill for about 5–8 minutes. Alternatively, put the kippers in a deep stoneware jug, tail uppermost, and pour over boiling water to cover. Leave to stand for 8–10 minutes, then drain. Serve with plenty of butter and hot toast.

**Aga cooking:** Cook the kippers with water and butter, as above, in the Roasting Oven for 5–8 minutes.

## all-in-one fry-up

Using a large frying pan, fry some sausages, then the bacon, then the tomato and mushrooms, keeping it all going in the same frying pan. When all of that is cooked and you are ready for eggs, make a space in the frying pan by pushing the cooked stuff around and crack in the eggs so that they sit amongst everything else. I try to add 3 or 4 eggs. Bring the pan to the table and let everyone help themselves – it doesn't matter if the eggs break as this is meant to be a friendly, informal fry-up! Serve with toast.

**Aga cooking:** Cook as above on the Boiling Plate.

# Saturday Lunch

## classic beef casserole with mashed potato topping

50ml red wine vinegar

700ml full-bodied red wine

200ml home-made beef stock

2 tbsp groundnut oil

1.75kg cubed chuck steak

2 large onions, peeled and chopped

1 tsp sugar

100g flour

150g button mushrooms

1 tin of good-quality plum tomatoes, drained

2 bay leaves

1 bunch of parsley, plus more for garnish

3 cloves of garlic, peeled

salt and pepper

MASHED POTATO TOPPING:

2.5kg large potatoes, peeled and cut into chunks

salt and pepper

250g butter

4 tbsp crème fraîche

1 The mashed potato topping can be made ahead of time. Fill a large saucepan with water, add salt and potatoes, bring up to the boil and boil for 10–12 minutes or until tender.

2 Drain the potatoes well. Using a potato ricer, mash the potatoes until smooth. Add the butter, crème fraîche and salt and pepper to taste. Beat well. Taste for seasoning.

3 Pour the red wine vinegar into a saucepan. Boil until it is almost all evaporated. Pour in the red wine and boil to reduce by half. Add the stock to the red wine and set aside.

4 Pre-heat the oven to 190ºC/375ºF/gas 5.

5 Using a large, heavy ovenproof pan, heat up the groundnut oil. Brown the meat pieces in batches and transfer them to a plate. Add the chopped onions and sugar to the pan and cook until they are charred at the edges and starting to colour.

6 Stir in the flour and scrape up all the sticky bits on the bottom, then add some of the reserved stock and wine and deglaze the pan. Return the beef to the pan and stir well. Add the mushrooms, tomatoes, herbs, garlic, salt, pepper and the remaining stock. Stir the saucepan and bring to the boil.

7 Put the pan into the oven and cook for 25 minutes, uncovered. Cover the pan with a lid, turn down the temperature to 150ºC/300ºF/gas 2 and continue to cook for another hour.

8 Take the casserole out of the oven and spoon the mashed potatoes on top. Return to the oven for another hour or so. To crisp up the top of the mash, grill for 2–3 minutes before serving garnished with parsley. (This casserole tastes even better if cooked the day before and reheated.)

**Aga cooking:** Cook the potatoes on the Boiling Plate for 3 minutes, then drain the water and transfer to the Simmering Oven for 20–25 minutes. Boil and reduce the red wine vinegar and red wine on the Boiling Plate. Brown the meat as above on the Boiling Plate or on the floor of the Roasting Oven. Cook the casserole in the Roasting Oven for 20–25 minutes, then cover and transfer to the Simmering Oven for 1–1½ hours.

# apple and custard pie

1kg cooking apples, peeled, cored and sliced

1 beaten egg yolk, for egg wash

**SWEET SHORTCRUST PASTRY:**

720g plain flour

240g caster sugar

pinch of salt

360g unsalted butter, cold and cubed

3 whole eggs, beaten

**PASTRY CREAM FILLING:**

200ml milk

1 vanilla pod or 1 tsp vanilla extract

1 whole egg

1 egg yolk

25g caster sugar

20g plain flour

**1** Sift the flour, sugar and salt into the food processor, then add the butter and process for 30 seconds. Add the eggs and process again just until it forms a ball (you may have to add a little cold water 1 tablespoon at a time if the mixture is dry). Wrap the pastry in clingfilm and rest in the fridge for a minimum of 30 minutes.

**2** Pre-heat the oven to 170°C/340°F/gas 3½. Line a 27-cm pie dish with the pastry. Line the pastry base with greaseproof paper and fill with baking beans. Blind-bake for 10 minutes, then set aside.

**3** Roll out the extra pastry to make a lid and refrigerate until you need it. (Any leftover pastry can be frozen in a ball.)

**4** To make the custard filling, pour the milk into a saucepan. If you are using a vanilla pod, slit it and scrape the seeds into the milk. Add the pod to a saucepan (or the vanilla extract, if using) and heat it gently.

**5** While it is warming, put the egg, egg yolk and caster sugar into the bowl of an electric mixer and whisk until it thickens. Sift in the flour and whisk until it is incorporated.

**6** Bring the milk up to a boil, and remove the pod if using one. With the whisk of the electric mixer still running (you may have to turn it down to prevent spattering), pour the boiling milk into the egg mix. Return the whole lot to the saucepan and continue to whisk until it becomes very thick. Remove it from the heat. Pour the pastry cream into a large bowl, cover the top with clingfilm and leave to cool. (You can make the cream the day before if you wish.)

**7** When the cream has cooled, spread it over the pastry case and lay the apple slices on top.

**8** Lay the rolled pastry lid over the apples, pinching the edges of the pie with your fingers. Make a little hole in the top for steam. Brush with the egg wash.

**9** Pre-heat the oven to 170°C/340°F/gas 3½. Bake the pie for 30 minutes or until the crust is golden. Serve cold or at room temperature.

**Aga cooking:** There is no need to blind-bake the pastry case. Heat the milk on the Simmering Plate. Bake the pie on the Roasting Oven floor with the cold plain shelf on the fourth set of runners for 35–40 minutes or until the crust is golden.

## sloe gin

2.2kg sloes, bullaces, damsons or even garden plums

700g unrefined golden caster sugar

thin peels of 2 organic oranges

1 bottle of gin or vodka

**1** Freeze the fruit in the freezer overnight (the fruits will burst which saves you the task of pricking them).

**2** Defrost the fruit and put it in a screw-top sterilised bottle or jar large enough to hold all the ingredients. Add the sugar and orange peel, then top up with the alcohol.

**3** Shake like mad, then leave to stand for 2 months or more, shaking the jar daily or whenever you think about it!

**4** After 2 months, strain it into clean, sterilised bottles or jars. Serve with Vacherin Mont d'Or cheese.

# Saturday Night Dinner Party

## roasted field mushrooms with goat's cheese and herbs

6 field mushrooms, stalks removed

olive oil

salt and pepper

knob of butter

1 large red onion, peeled and finely chopped

1 tsp golden caster sugar

150g mixed wild mushrooms, cut in half or smaller if very large or left whole if small

2 cloves of garlic, peeled and crushed

1 tbsp lemon thyme leaves

juice of ½ a lemon, plus the zest

150g goat's cheese, crumbled

**1** Pre-heat the oven to 190ºC/375ºF/gas 5.

**2** Lay the field mushrooms on a large shallow baking tray, drizzle over some olive oil and season with salt and pepper. Slide the tray into the oven and cook for about 10–15 minutes or until they are just soft.

**3** Heat up about 1 tablespoon of olive oil and the knob of butter in a frying pan. Add the red onion and sugar and cook until soft and caramelised, then add the wild mushrooms, garlic, lemon thyme, salt and pepper and juice and zest of the lemon. Don't let the garlic burn. Cook for 5–8 minutes, or until the mushrooms are tender.

**4** Take the field mushrooms out of the oven and put one on each plate. Spoon some of the wild mushroom mix onto the field mushrooms and scatter over the crumbled goat's cheese. Garnish with a few more thyme leaves. Serve with crusty bread.

**Aga cooking:** Cook the mushrooms in the Roasting Oven for 10 minutes. Cook the onion and the rest of the topping as above on the Boiling or Simmering Plate.

# rack of veal with mustard herb crust

**1 red onion, peeled and chopped**

**1 clove of garlic, peeled**

**2 tbsp fresh thyme**

**3 tbsp Dijon mustard**

**1 tbsp green peppercorns in brine, drained**

**3 tbsp butter**

**salt**

**6 tbsp fresh breadcrumbs**

**1 rack of veal (approximately 2.5–3kg), French trimmed, skin and fat removed, allowing for 1 rib per person**

**1** Pre-heat the oven to 200ºC/400ºF/gas 6. Put the roasting tin into the oven to heat up.

**2** Put the onion, garlic, thyme, mustard, green peppercorns, butter, and salt into a food processor. Whiz until everything is all thoroughly chopped and combined. Remove the blade and mix in the breadcrumbs. Set aside.

**3** Remove the tin from the oven. Place the veal in the tin and cook for 10 minutes, then remove from the oven and press the breadcrumb mixture onto the veal. Continue cooking for a further 10–12 minutes or until golden and crusty. Serve with crushed potatoes and spinach.

**Aga cooking:** Cook as above in the Roasting Oven.

# crushed potatoes

**10–12 large potatoes, peeled and cut into chunks**

**salt and pepper**

**100g butter**

**2–4 tbsp olive oil**

**1** Fill a large saucepan with water (or milk, for extra richness), add salt and potatoes and bring up to a boil and cook for 12–15 minutes or until they are soft and tender. Drain.

**2** Instead of mashing the potatoes, crush them with the back of the fork – they will not and should not be smooth. Stir in the butter and olive oil and season to taste. These potatoes can be made ahead of time and reheated if you wish.

**Aga cooking:** Boil for 3–4 minutes on the Boiling Plate, then drain off the water and cover with a lid. Place in the Simmering Oven for 20 minutes until the potatoes are tender.

# leek and potato cakes with cheese sauce

(vegetarian main course alternative)

**6 leeks, finely sliced**

**4–6 potatoes, depending on size, peeled**

**2 eggs, beaten**

**100g Parmesan cheese, grated**

**salt and white pepper**

**1 tbsp Dijon mustard**

**CHEESE SAUCE:**

**40g butter**

**20g plain flour**

**425ml warm milk**

**180g Parmesan or Gruyère cheese, finely grated**

**salt and pepper**

**1** Bring a saucepan of water up to the boil, add the leeks and cook for 1 minute. Drain well and set aside.

**2** Grate the potatoes and give them a good squeeze to get rid of as much liquid as possible. Add them to the leeks and stir in the rest of the ingredients. Shape them into cakes and put onto a plate lined with kitchen paper. (You can prepare them up to this point 24 hours in advance and refrigerate, if you wish.)

**3** Pre-heat the oven to 180ºC/350ºF/gas 5. Line a shallow baking tray with Bake-O-Glide and lightly brush it with some flavourless oil. Slide the tray into the oven and heat it up for a few minutes.

**4** Place the cakes on the tray and cook them in the oven for 10–12 minutes per side or until they are golden. Remove them from the oven and leave to stand for a few minutes. Alternatively, fry the cakes in a frying pan on the hob. Do them in batches and keep them warm.

**5** Meanwhile, make the cheese sauce. Melt the butter in a small saucepan. Add the flour to the butter and stir well with a wooden spoon until it turns into a glossy paste. Gradually pour in the warm milk, a little at a time, stirring or whisking all the time until all the milk is incorporated and you have a smooth sauce. Simmer the sauce for 3–5 minutes, whisking occasionally, so that the flour is cooked. Do not let the sauce burn or catch on the bottom.

**6** Remove the sauce from the heat and stir in the cheese. Taste for seasoning. Cover the surface of the sauce with clingfilm to prevent a skin forming.

**7** When cooked, serve the cakes with the cheese sauce.

**Aga cooking:** Cook the leeks on the Boiling Plate. Heat up the tray in the Roasting Oven. Cook the cakes as above on the Roasting Oven floor for 8–10 minutes per side. Make the cheese sauce on the Simmering Plate.

*leek and potato cakes with cheese sauce*

# passionfruit meringue

**MERINGUE:**

**6 large egg whites, without a trace of egg yolk**

**350g golden caster sugar**

**2 tsp white wine vinegar**

**1½ tsp cornflour**

**TOPPING:**

**300 double or whipping cream**

**12–14 passionfruit, really ripe and wrinkled**

**1 pomegranate**

**toasted coconut shavings, to serve**

**1** Pre-heat the oven to 150°C/300°F/gas 2. Line a flat baking tray or a tarte tatin dish with Bake-O-Glide.

**2** Put the egg whites into the bowl of an electric mixer – the bowl must be scrupulously clean. Whisk the egg whites together until they reach the soft peak stage – shiny and thick – then add the sugar 2 tablespoons at a time until it is really thick and glossy. Gently fold the vinegar and cornflour into the egg whites. Spread the mix onto the baking tray, shaping it into a circle 25cm in diameter, spreading it out from the middle.

**3** Bake for 1 hour, then turn off the oven and leave to cool in the oven.

**4** Transfer to a serving dish – the meringue will be uncooperative and may even start to break up, but don't worry as that's all part of its deliciousness. Cover with clingfilm or large airtight tin. (The meringue can be made the day before up to this stage.)

**5** Whip the cream to soft peaks and spread on top of the meringue base. Cut the passionfruit in half and squeeze over the cream. Cut the pomegranate in half and, holding the cut side down over the meringue, tap the back of it with a wooden spoon so the seeds shower down. Serve with toasted coconut shavings.

**Aga cooking:** Slide the meringue onto the third set of runners in the Simmering Oven (for 4-oven Aga cookers, use the middle runners) and bake for 30–40 minutes.

# fig florentines

50g unsalted butter

50g golden caster sugar

50g dried figs, chopped

25g mixed peel

50g pistachio nuts, chopped

25g flaked almonds

150g good-quality dark chocolate

**1** Pre-heat the oven to 180°C/350°F/gas 4. Line a shallow baking tray with Bake-O-Glide.

**2** Melt the butter and sugar in a saucepan. Bring it slowly up to the boil to dissolve the sugar. Add the figs, mixed peel and nuts and stir well.

**3** Drop teaspoonfuls onto the prepared tray and press them down (this quantity will make 12–15 florentines). Space well apart.

**4** Bake the florentines for 8–10 minutes or until they are golden. Do not let them burn.

**5** Cool them for a minute on the tray, then move to a wire rack. Leave to cool completely.

**6** When the florentines are completely cool, melt the chocolate and spread over the underside. Leave to set, chocolate side up. Serve with coffee. They can be stored in an airtight tin for 3–4 days.

**Aga cooking:** Melt the butter and sugar on the Simmering Plate. Slide the tray onto the fourth set of runners in the Roasting Oven with the cold plain shelf directly above. Bake for 5–8 minutes or until golden. For 4-oven Aga cookers, bake on the third set of runners in the Baking Oven for 8–10 minutes or until golden.

# Sunday Breakfast

## coddled eggs and soldiers

**PER PERSON:**
**butter**
**1 egg**
**salt and pepper**

**1** Pre-heat the oven to 180°C/350°F/gas 4.

**2** Butter the inside of the egg coddler (you will need one per person). Crack the egg into the coddler and season with salt and pepper. Seal the lid on the coddler.

**3** Put the coddler into a deep roasting tin and pour boiling water into the tin so that it comes halfway up the side of the coddler.

**4** Put the tin in the oven and cook the eggs for 3–5 minutes or until they are lightly cooked. Serve with toast soldiers.

**Aga cooking:** Cook as above in the Roasting Oven.

## fried puffball with bacon

**1 medium-sized puffball**
**12 rashers of good-quality bacon**
**knob of unsalted butter**
**6 slices of Gruyère cheese**

**1** Slice the puffball into six thickish slices.

**2** Cook the bacon in a frying pan, then transfer to a warmed dish and keep warm.

**3** Using the same pan, cook the puffball slices in the bacon fat, adding a little butter if necessary.

**4** When the puffball is ready, top each slice with a couple of rashers of bacon and a slice of cheese.

**5** Pre-heat the grill and grill for 2–4 minutes or until the cheese starts to melt. Serve with hot toast. This is also good served with a fried egg on top.

**Aga cooking:** Cook the bacon on the Boiling or Simmering Plate. Melt the cheese on the first set of runners in the Roasting Oven.

# Sunday Lunch

## bloody mary

475ml vodka or dry sherry

1 litre tomato juice or clamato juice

100ml passata

dash of Worcestershire Sauce, to taste

juice of 1 lemon

dash of Tabasco sauce

2½ tsp prepared horseradish, or freshly grated if you can get it (optional)

celery salt, to taste

6 celery sticks with leaves, for stirring

**1** Combine everything except the celery sticks in a large jug with some ice and stir vigorously.

**2** Strain and pour into glasses with fresh ice. Garnish with a celery stick.

## roast pheasant with savoury breadcrumbs

4 bay leaves

3 red onions, peeled and quartered

4 oven-ready pheasants

salt and pepper

75 g butter, softened

splash of Marsala wine

300ml good-quality game or chicken stock

**SAVOURY BREADCRUMBS:**

1–1½ tbsp good-quality olive oil

25g butter (clarified butter is best, see page 158)

2 shallots, peeled and finely chopped or even minced (a microplane grater is perfect for this job)

8 tbsp sourdough breadcrumbs

1 tbsp walnuts, chopped, or pine nuts

1 tbsp raisins, soaked in boiling water

**1** Pre-heat the oven to 190ºC/375ºF/gas 5.

**2** Put a bay leaf and a piece of red onion into each pheasant cavity and season with salt and pepper. Smear the butter over each bird and season with salt and pepper. Put the remaining onion quarters on the bottom of a large roasting tin. Place the pheasants on the onions.

**3** Cook the pheasants for 1 hour or until the juices run clear when the thigh is poked with a skewer.

**4** Meanwhile, make the savoury breadcrumbs. Heat the oil and butter in a frying pan and add the shallots, breadcrumbs and nuts. Toss everything together over a medium heat until the breadcrumbs have absorbed all the fat and the mix is crisp and golden. Drain on kitchen paper. Store in a sealed bag or tin. When ready to use, drain the raisins from the water and toss into the breadcrumbs.

**5** Remove the birds from the oven. Lift out each bird and carefully tip them so that any juices run into the pan juices. Move the birds to a warmed plate, cover with foil and rest while you make the gravy.

**6** Skim off excess fat from the tin. Deglaze the tin with the Marsala. Add the stock. Bring it to the boil on the hob, then simmer for 2–3 minutes.

**7** Pour the gravy into a warmed jug. Taste for seasoning. Carve the pheasants and serve with the gravy and savoury breadcrumbs.

**Aga cooking:** Cook the pheasants on the third set of runners in the Roasting Oven for 1 hour. Make the savoury breadcrumbs on the Simmering Plate. Deglaze the pan as above on the Simmering Plate.

# rosemary-infused chestnuts

**240g vacuum-packed whole chestnuts**

**olive oil**

**1 sprig of organic rosemary**

**1** Put the whole chestnuts into a saucepan and cover with olive oil and add the rosemary. Heat up very gently so that they are warmed through – do not let the oil boil.

**2** Remove from the heat and leave to infuse for about 15 minutes. Drain with a slotted spoon and serve with the roast pheasant (see page 101).

**Aga cooking:** Cook as above on the Simmering Plate.

# game chips

**6–7 potatoes, peeled**

**beef dripping or sunflower oil, for frying**

**salt**

**1** Slice the potatoes on a mandolin so they are about the thickness of a crisp – in other words, very thin. Soak them in cold water for 10 minutes and drain well. Dry them really well.

**2** Use a deep fat fryer if you have one, or use a heavy-bottomed pan. Heat up the dripping or oil – it should be about 5–6cm deep when melted. Test that the fat is hot enough by throwing in a breadcrumb and see if it sizzles. Fry the game chips in batches.

**3** Drain on kitchen paper, sprinkle with salt and keep them warm. Serve with the roast pheasant (see page 101). (These can be made in advance if you wish.)

**Aga cooking:** Cook as above on the Boiling or Simmering Plate.

# bread sauce

**500ml milk**

**2 whole cloves**

**1 medium onion, peeled and finely chopped**

**salt and pepper**

**150g stale white breadcrumbs, or more if needed**

**30ml thick double cream**

**40g butter, softened**

**1** Put the milk, cloves, chopped onion and salt and pepper into a saucepan and simmer for 10–15 minutes until the onion is soft.

**2** Take the pan off the heat and let it infuse for an hour or longer.

**3** Just before serving, remove the cloves and sprinkle in the breadcrumbs – the breadcrumbs will swell after a while but you don't want a sauce that is too thick so don't be too quick to add more breadcrumbs. Stir in the cream and butter. Pour into a warmed bowl and serve with the roast pheasant.

**Aga cooking:** Cook as above on the Simmering Plate.

# wild rice and wild mushroom stuffing

**250g wild rice**

**1 large red onion, peeled and chopped**

**150g wild mushrooms, cleaned and chopped**

**2 tbsp olive oil**

**200g pack chestnuts, halved**

**80g butter, softened**

**2 heaped tbsp freshly chopped flat leaf parsley**

**salt and pepper**

**1** Cook the rice according to the instructions until tender but still with a bite.

**2** While the rice is cooking, cook the onion and the mushrooms in the olive oil in a frying pan until soft and translucent. Set aside.

**3** Pre-heat the oven to 180ºC/350ºF/gas 4.

**4** When the rice is ready, drain off all excess water and tip into a large bowl. Stir in the onion, mushrooms and the remaining ingredients. Butter an ovenproof dish, put the stuffing into it and cover with foil. Bake for 25–30 minutes.

**Aga cooking:** Put the rice, water and salt into a large saucepan and bring to the boil on the Boiling Plate. Stir once, then cover with a lid and place on the Simmering Oven floor for 18–20 minutes. Cook the onion and mushrooms as above on the Simmering Plate. Cook the stuffing in the Roasting Oven for 20–25 minutes.

# plum and hazelnut crumble

1kg plums, stones removed and cut into quarters

240g plain flour

240g very cold unsalted butter

240g golden granulated sugar

½ tsp cinnamon

100g chopped hazelnuts

soft brown sugar, for the final topping

chocolate shavings (optional)

**1** Pre-heat the oven to 190ºC/375ºF/gas 5.

**2** Butter an ovenproof dish. Put the fruit into the dish.

**3** In a roomy bowl, sift in the flour and rub in the butter. When the mix resembles coarse breadcrumbs, mix in the sugar, cinnamon and chopped hazelnuts (you can do this in an electric mixer but don't over-do it). Spoon the crumble topping over the fruit and sprinkle over some soft brown sugar.

**4** Put the dish into a roasting tin and cook in the oven for 35–40 minutes.

**5** If you wish, sprinkle chocolate shavings over the crumble when it comes out of the oven.

**Aga cooking:** Put the dish into a roasting tin and hang the tin on the fourth set of runners in the Roasting Oven. Cook for 20–25 minutes, then transfer to the Simmering Oven and cook for a further 20–25 minutes or until the fruit is tender and the topping is cooked. For 4-oven Aga cookers, cook on the third set of runners in the Baking Oven for 35–45 minutes.

# Sunday Tea

## treacle sponge cake

175g self-raising flour

175g soft unsalted butter

95g dark muscovado sugar

80g golden syrup

1 tbsp milk

1 tsp ground ginger

pinch of cinnamon

3 large organic eggs

1 rounded tsp baking powder

FILLING:

150g golden icing sugar, plus more for dusting

75g unsalted butter

**1** Pre-heat the oven to 170ºC/340ºF/gas 3½. Line two 20cm loose-bottomed cake tins with Bake-O-Glide.

**2** Put all the cake ingredients into the bowl of an electric mixer and beat with the beater attachment until combined. Divide the mixture between the tins.

**3** Bake the cakes for 30–35 minutes or until golden on top, gently coming away from the sides and spring back when lightly pressed on top.

**4** Remove the cakes from the oven and stand on a wire rack for a minute, then remove them from the tin and cool on the wire rack.

**5** When the cakes are cool, beat the golden icing sugar and butter together and spread onto one cake, then top with the second cake. Dust with more golden icing sugar and serve.

**Aga cooking:** Place the grid shelf on the floor of the Roasting Oven and place the cake tins to the right on the grid shelf. Slide the cold plain shelf onto the third set of runners and bake the cakes for 20 minutes or until golden on top, gently coming away from the sides and spring back when lightly pressed on top. For 4-oven Aga cookers, cook the cakes on the fourth set of runners in the Baking Oven and use the cold plain shelf only if the cakes are browning too quickly.

*plum and hazelnut crumble*

# Winter House Party serves 6

PANCAKES WITH MAPLE BUTTER

BAKERY BASKET

## SUNDAY BREAKFAST

SCRAMBLED EGGS WITH
SMOKED SALMON AND
BRIOCHE

BAKERY BASKET

## SATURDAY LUNCH

FABULOUS FISH PIE

AFFOGATO COFFEE ICE CREAM
FLOATS

## SUNDAY LUNCH

ROAST PORK WITH
CALVADOS GRAVY

BLACK PUDDING AND
APPLE STUFFING

GOLDEN SYRUP PUDDING

## FRIDAY NIGHT SUPPER

TANDOORI ROASTED
CHICKEN

MANGO AND LIME RICE
PUDDING

## SATURDAY NIGHT
DINNER PARTY

CRAB BISQUE

FILLET OF BEEF WRAPPED
IN PASTRY

VEGETARIAN ALTERNATIVE:
PENNE GORGONZOLA BAKE

PAVLOVA WITH GRIOTTINE
CHERRIES AND ALMONDS

## SUNDAY TEA

CINNAMON TOAST

# Friday Night Supper

## tandoori roasted chicken

**3kg organic free-range chicken**
**150–200ml chicken stock**

**MARINADE:**
**400ml Greek yoghurt**
**1½ tsp turmeric**
**1 heaped tbsp garam masala**
**3cm piece of ginger, grated**
**1–2 red chillies, seeds removed**
**1 clove of garlic, peeled**
**juice of 1 organic lemon**
**salt and pepper**
**slick of sunflower oil – about 2 tbsp**

1 Whiz the marinade ingredients together in a food processor, adding a little water if it is too thick. Taste for seasoning.

2 Put the chicken into a resealable plastic bag. Pour over the marinade and massage it into the chicken. Seal the bag and marinate the chicken overnight in the fridge.

3 When you are ready to cook the chicken, remove it from the fridge at least 20 minutes beforehand to allow it to come to room temperature. Pre-heat the oven to 180ºC/350ºF/gas 4.

4 Put the chicken into a roasting tin and pour over the marinade. Cook the chicken for about 1–1½ hours or until the juices run clear from the thigh. Check the chicken halfway through the cooking time and add stock if it is a bit dry. Baste the chicken with the marinade frequently. If the chicken is browning too quickly, cover with foil.

5 Remove the chicken from the oven, transfer to a warmed platter and cover with foil. Rest for 15 minutes.

6 While the chicken is resting, skim off the fat from the roasting tin, then bring the sauce back to the boil. Add any resting juices to the sauce and taste. If you need to, add a little chicken stock and deglaze the tin with that. Adjust the seasoning with lemon juice or salt.

7 Carve the chicken onto a warm serving plate and spoon over some of the sauce and serve with wedges of lemon, poppadoms, naan bread, basmati rice, mango chutney and Greek yoghurt.

**Aga cooking:** Cook the chicken in the Roasting Oven for 45–60 minutes or until the juices run clear from the thigh. Baste the chicken with the marinade frequently. If the chicken is browning too much, cover with the cold plain shelf. Reheat the sauce on the Boiling Plate.

# mango and lime rice pudding

**RICE PUDDING:**

**200g pudding rice**

**60g caster sugar**

**600ml milk**

**600ml coconut milk**

**LIME SYRUP:**

**juice and zest of 8 limes**

**200g granulated sugar**

**GARNISH:**

**3 mangoes, peeled and stoned, 1 very thinly sliced, 2 diced into tiny pieces**

**30g desiccated coconut**

**1** Pre-heat the oven to 150ºC/300ºF/gas 2.

**2** Place all the rice pudding ingredients in a large ovenproof pan and bring to the boil, then transfer to the oven for 35–40 minutes or until tender.

**3** Remove the rice pudding from the oven and leave to cool. Store in the fridge. This can all be done the day before.

**4** To make the syrup, put all the ingredients into a small saucepan with 200ml water and bring to the boil. Turn down the heat and simmer for 5–10 minutes or until it starts to thicken slightly. Remove from the heat and leave to cool completely. Pour into a jug and store in the refrigerator. The syrup can be made the day before if you wish.

**5** Remove the rice pudding from the fridge 15 minutes before you want to serve it and stir in the diced mango. Spoon the rice pudding into individual bowls and garnish with some sliced mango and the coconut and drizzle over some of the lime syrup. Serve cold.

**Aga cooking:** Cook the rice pudding in the Simmering Oven for 1–1½ hours. Cook the sauce as above on the Simmering Plate.

# Saturday Breakfast

## pancakes with maple butter

**145g plain flour**

**1 tbsp caster sugar**

**1 tsp baking powder**

**pinch of salt**

**1 whole large egg**

**175–200ml milk or buttermilk**

**30ml sunflower oil or melted butter**

**1 tsp vanilla extract**

**MAPLE BUTTER:**

**500g unsalted butter, at room temperature**

**3–4 tbsp maple syrup**

**1** To make the maple butter, whiz up the butter and maple syrup in a food processor or electric mixer until smooth. Taste as you go, adding more maple syrup if it needs it. Spoon the butter into a serving dish and refrigerate until 1 hour before serving.

**2** Put all the pancake ingredients into a bowl and mix well with a whisk, so there are no lumps. (You may need a little less or a little more milk or buttermilk, depending on how thick you like your pancakes and what the flour is like.)

**3** Heat a little oil in a frying pan over a medium heat and cook the pancakes in batches.

**4** Serve straight away with maple butter, and with streaky bacon if you wish. This recipe makes about 16 small pancakes. If you want to double the recipe, do so.

**Aga cooking:** Place a piece of Bake-O-Glide on the Simmering Plate and grease with a little oil. Cook the pancakes in batches. Spoon some of the pancake mix onto the hot surface and cook until it starts to bubble. Flip the pancake over and cook for 2 minutes or until puffed up.

*pancakes and maple butter*

# Saturday Lunch

## fabulous fish pie

**250g undyed smoked haddock, chopped into small pieces**

**650g cod, cut into small pieces**

**8 scallops, sliced in half horizontally**

**16 tiger prawns, shelled and vein removed**

**4 hard-boiled eggs, peeled and cut into wedges**

**2 heaped tbsp freshly chopped flat leaf parsley, plus extra to garnish**

**zest and juice of 1 lemon**

**salt and pepper**

**30g butter**

**30g flour**

**450ml hot milk**

**30ml double cream**

**½ onion, peeled and quartered**

**MASHED POTATO TOPPING:**

**900g potatoes, peeled and cut into chunks**

**generous knob of butter**

**120ml sour cream or crème fraîche**

**salt and pepper**

**30g Gruyère cheese, grated**

**1** First, make the mashed potato topping. Put the potatoes into a saucepan of salted water and boil for 10–12 minutes or until tender. Drain well. Put them through a potato ricer until they are creamy and fluffy. Beat in the butter and sour cream and season with salt and pepper. Set aside.

**2** Butter a large, deep, ovenproof dish. Put all the fish and seafood into the dish and add the egg, parsley and lemon zest. Season.

**3** Next, make the sauce. Melt the butter in a saucepan and add the flour, stirring all the time. When all the flour has been absorbed into the butter, slowly add the milk little by little, stirring constantly. When all the milk has been used, add the lemon juice. You should have a smooth white sauce. Pour in the cream and season. Simmer the sauce for 3–4 minutes so that it is slightly thicker and glossy.

**4** When it is ready, pour it over the fish. Mix it all in really well so that everything is coated with the sauce.

**5** Spread the mashed potato over the fish and make a pattern using a fork, then sprinkle over the cheese. The pie can be made to this point 24 hours in advance. Remove the pie from the fridge 20 minutes before cooking to bring to room temperature.

**6** Pre-heat the oven to 190°C/375°F/gas 5. Cook for 35–45 minutes. The top of the pie should be crispy, bubbling and enticingly browned. Serve garnished with parsley and with peas.

**Aga cooking:** Cook the potatoes on the Boiling Plate for 3 minutes, then drain the water and transfer to the Simmering Oven for 20–25 minutes. Make the sauce on the Simmering Plate. Cook the pie on the third set of runners in the Roasting Oven for 35–45 minutes.

## affogato coffee ice cream floats

**PER PERSON:**

**1 scoop of really good-quality vanilla ice cream**

**1 shot of hot espresso (you will need an espresso maker for this)**

1 Put a scoop of ice cream into each bowl or coffee cup and pour over a shot of espresso. Serve straight away.

2 If you wish to get ahead with this dish, scoop ice cream balls onto a tray lined with greaseproof paper and open freeze them. When you are ready to assemble, just take the scoops of ice cream out of the freezer and pop them into the dishes.

# Saturday Night Dinner Party

## crab bisque

**olive oil**

**500g onions, peeled and chopped**

**1 large cooked crab, about 2.5kg including shell, meat removed, white meat separated from the brown and chopped up**

**1kg tomatoes, chopped**

**150ml white wine**

**6-8 sprigs of fresh tarragon**

**zest of 1 organic lemon**

**1 clove of garlic, peeled**

**salt and pepper**

**175ml double cream, warmed**

1 Put a little olive oil into a deep saucepan and cook the onions until soft.

2 Add the brown crab meat, tomatoes, 1 litre of water, wine, herbs, lemon zest, garlic and a little salt and pepper. Bring it to the boil, then turn the heat down and simmer for 15–20 minutes.

3 Strain through a sieve lined with muslin. Just before you are ready to serve, re-heat the soup and add the flaked white meat and the warmed cream. Taste, adjust the seasoning and serve with water biscuits.

**Aga cooking:** Cook the onions as above on the Simmering Plate, then add the remaining brown meat and other ingredients and cook in the Simmering Oven for 15–20 minutes.

# fillet of beef wrapped in pastry

1 tbsp sunflower oil

1kg fillet of beef, trimmed

3 shallots, peeled and very finely chopped

500g mix of wild mushrooms, very finely chopped

1 clove of garlic, peeled and crushed

salt and pepper

splash of red wine vinegar

1 tbsp freshly chopped flat leaf parsley

500–700g pack of good-quality puff pastry

1 packet of ready-made crêpes, or make your own – you will need 3 or 4 crêpes

2–4 tbsp Dijon mustard

olive oil

egg wash – one egg beaten with some milk

1 Heat the sunflower oil in a large pan and seal the fillet on all sides. Remove the fillet and set aside.

2 Cook the shallots in a little oil in the same pan until soft. Add the mushrooms and cook for a few minutes then add the garlic, salt and pepper and a splash of red wine vinegar. Continue cooking until the mushrooms are soft and the vinegar has evaporated. Stir in the parsley. Check for seasoning and set aside to cool. You can refrigerate until required.

3 When you are ready to assemble and cook the dish, roll out the pastry out into a rectangle. Line a shallow baking sheet with Bake-O-Glide and lay the pastry on it. Lay the crêpes along the centre. Spread some mustard along the centre of the crêpes. Season with salt and pepper, then spread the mushrooms on top.

4 Lay the fillet on the mushrooms and spread with more mustard. Brush the pastry with egg wash and carefully wrap up the meat like a parcel, long side up and over then short sides, using the egg wash as 'glue'. Turn the parcel over so the seam side is underneath. (You can leave it like this in the fridge for up to 3 hours.)

5 When you are ready to cook the beef, bring it back to room temperature. Pre-heat the oven to 180ºC/350ºF/gas 4.

6 Brush the pastry with more egg wash. Cook the meat for 20–25 minutes (check it after 15 minutes and cover with foil if it is browning too much). This will give you a rare fillet. The pastry should be golden.

7 Rest for 10–12 minutes, then carve and serve. You will need to carve it in thick slices. Serve with braised leeks and roasted root vegetables.

Aga cooking: Seal the fillet as above on the Simmering Plate. Cook on the fourth set of runners in the Roasting Oven for 25 minutes – check after 15 minutes and slide the cold plain shelf onto the second set of runners if it browns too quickly. Cook until golden on top.

## penne gorgonzola bake (vegetarian main course alternative)

500g penne pasta

3 garlic cloves, peeled

salt

250ml double cream

50g Parmesan cheese, grated

125g Gorgonzola cheese, cubed

85g unsalted butter, cut into cubes

4 ciabatta crispbreads, crumbled

1 Pre-heat the oven to 180°C/350°F/gas 4.

2 Bring a large pan of water up to the boil. Add the pasta, garlic cloves and salt to the water. Cook for 10 minutes or until the pasta is tender.

3 Remove the garlic and 3 tbsp of cooking water to a saucepan and set aside. Drain the pasta and put into a buttered ovenproof dish.

4 Add the cream to the garlic and water, bring back to the boil and reduce until thick. Mash the garlic with a potato masher and add both cheeses. Pour the creamy sauce over the pasta and top with the butter cubes.

5 Bake for 20–25 minutes or until crispy and golden, then sprinkle over the crumbled crispbreads and serve.

**Aga cooking:** Cook the pasta on the Boiling Plate. Cook the cream and garlic as above on the Boiling Plate, then cook as above in the Roasting Oven for 20–25 minutes.

## pavlova with griottine cherries and almonds

MERINGUE:

6 large egg whites (without a trace of egg yolk)

350g golden caster sugar

2 tsp white wine vinegar

1½ tsp cornflour

TOPPING:

300ml double or whipping cream

150ml griottine cherries

80g toasted sliced almonds

1 Pre-heat the oven to 150°C/300°F/gas 2. Line a flat baking tray or a tarte tatin dish with Bake-O-Glide.

2 Put the egg whites into the bowl of an electric mixer – the bowl must be scrupulously clean. Whisk the egg whites together until they reach the soft peak stage – shiny and thick – then add the sugar 2 tablespoons at a time until it is really thick and glossy. Gently fold the vinegar and cornflour into the egg whites. Spread the mix onto the baking tray, shaping it into a circle with a 25-cm diameter, spreading it out from the middle.

3 Bake in the oven for 1 hour, then turn off the oven and leave to cool completely.

4 Transfer to a serving dish – the meringue will be uncooperative and may even start to break up, but don't worry as that's all part of its attraction.

5 Whip the cream to soft peaks and fill the pavlova with it. Scatter over the cherries, a little of their liquid and the toasted almonds.

**Aga cooking:** Slide the baking tray onto the third set of runners in the Simmering Oven (for 4-oven Aga cookers, use the middle runners) and bake for 30–40 minutes, then transfer to a wire rack to cool.

# Sunday Breakfast

## scrambled eggs with smoked salmon and brioche

15 eggs

180ml whipping cream

75g unsalted butter

450g smoked salmon trimmings, chopped into pieces

black pepper

6–8 slices of brioche, toasted

**1** Crack the eggs into a glass bowl. Add the whipping cream and beat the eggs gently.

**2** Melt half the butter in a large non-stick pan, then pour in the eggs. Stir the eggs constantly with a wooden fork or spoon until they just start to form soft curds.

**3** Remove from the heat and add the smoked salmon, black pepper and the rest of the butter. Stir in, making sure it is still wet and soft. Serve straight away with toasted brioche. (It helps to have someone else on hand to toast the brioche while you make the eggs.)

**Aga cooking:** Cook as above on the Simmering Plate.

# Sunday Lunch

## roast pork with calvados gravy

2.5kg pork joint (ideally rib roast with the loin and plenty of fat)

3 onions, peeled and cut in half

1 apple, peeled, cored and chopped

2 carrots, peeled and roughly chopped

3 sprigs of fresh sage

salt and pepper

GRAVY:

2 tbsp flour

50ml Calvados

500ml–1 litre stock or water from cooked vegetables

1 tsp apple jelly

salt and pepper

1  The day before, leave the pork to dry out overnight in the fridge, uncovered. (The secret to getting the crackling really crispy is to start off with very dry skin. If you are keeping the skin on the joint, leave it in the fridge for 24 hours patted dry with a piece of kitchen paper and uncovered.)

2  Pre-heat the oven to 200°C/400°F/gas 6.

3  Score the skin on the meat with a very sharp knife, with the cuts 1cm apart. Line a large roasting tin with Bake-O-Glide and spread out the onions, apple, carrots and sage on the bottom of the tin. Lay the pork on top.

4  Cook for 1 hour, then turn the oven down to 160°C/325°F/gas 3 and continue to cook for another 1½–2 hours or until done. Cover the meat loosely with foil and rest for 15 minutes.

5  Meanwhile, make the gravy. Remove all but 2 tablespoons of fat from the tin. Do not remove the vegetables. Sprinkle in the flour and stir well so that it absorbs all of the fat. Pour in the Calvados and bring to the boil until it has almost evaporated, then pour in the stock or vegetable water (the quantity depends on how thick you like your gravy). Add the apple jelly. Bring the gravy up to a rapid simmer and cook for 5 minutes. Season and reduce until it has reached the consistency you like. Strain it into a jug and keep warm.

Aga cooking: Roast the pork in the Roasting Oven for 1 hour, then transfer to the Simmering Oven and continue to cook for 2–2½ hours. Make the gravy on the Simmering Plate.

## black pudding and apple stuffing

2 large onions, peeled and chopped

550g Boudin Noir or black pudding (Boudin Noir is French black pudding and is higher in fat than black pudding; if you use black pudding you may want to increase the butter quantity)

100g soft butter, plus 25g butter, diced

2 apples, peeled, cored and chopped

2 tbsp finely chopped fresh sage leaves

splash of Calvados

200g sourdough breadcrumbs

salt and pepper

1  Pre-heat the oven to 180°C/350°F/gas 5. Butter an ovenproof dish.

2  Put the onions into a saucepan with 300ml water and bring to the boil. Gently simmer until the onions are soft. Drain and transfer the onions to a large mixing bowl and set aside.

3  In a large frying pan, cook the black pudding. Remove the black pudding with a slotted spoon and mix with the onions.

4  Gently heat up the butter and cook the apple with the sage in the pan until soft, then deglaze the pan with a splash of Calvados. Mix in the onions, black pudding, breadcrumbs, apples and 100g butter. Season with salt and pepper. Pile into the buttered dish and dot with the diced butter. Cook for 35–40 minutes.

Aga cooking: Cook the onions and black pudding as above on the Simmering Plate. Cook the stuffing in the Roasting Oven for 35–40 minutes.

## golden syrup pudding

**65–85g unsalted butter, softened**

**8–10 slices bread, cut to medium thickness**

**8–10 tbsp golden syrup**

**500ml milk**

**500ml double cream**

**6 eggs**

**1** Pre-heat the oven to 180°C/350°F/gas 4. Butter an ovenproof dish.

**2** Spread each slice of bread with some butter, remove the crusts and cut into soldiers.

**3** Pour the golden syrup into the bottom of the ovenproof dish and layer the bread on top to make slightly overlapping layers.

**4** Beat the milk, cream and eggs together well and pour over the bread.

**5** Put the dish on a shallow baking tray and cook for 20–25 minutes. Check it halfway through cooking – it should still have a bit of a wobble to it when it is removed. Serve warm with vanilla ice cream.

**Aga cooking:** Cook on the third set of runners in the Roasting Oven for 20 minutes or until it is puffed up and golden.

# Sunday Tea

## cinnamon toast

**150g soft butter**

**1 tsp ground cinnamon**

**1 small loaf of delicious bread, cut into slices (not too thick)**

**1** Put the butter and cinnamon into a bowl and beat until it is all well blended.

**2** Toast the bread. Spread the toast with the cinnamon butter and serve while still hot.

**Aga cooking:** Use the Aga toasting rack.

*golden syrup pudding*

**high days and holidays**

There are certain times of the year when you have to entertain, such as Christmas, birthdays and other milestone events that need to be marked by a party, and other occasions when you will want any excuse for a knees-up.

**planning**

The rules of engagement for a big bash are organisation, confidence in your ingredients, simplicity and elegance. Successful cooking and entertaining is all about confidence – the more you do it, the better you will become and the easier it will be. First, decide what sort of party it is to be and look at the space you have available. If you intend to hold the party outside, in the summer months you will need a wet-weather plan, and in the winter months a marquee with heaters.

**tips**

Before you decide on a menu full of expensive ingredients, set an overall budget taking everything into account, including:

- Decorations, such as flowers for the table and rooms
- Table and chair hire if you don't have enough
- Cutlery and crockery hire
- Food costs
- Drinks – spirits, wines and soft drinks
- Staff
- Marquee hire, heaters, etc.

When it comes to entertaining for traditional holidays like Christmas, take a deep breath and get as much cooking done in advance as possible. Start planning and ordering early, as everyone else will be planning for the same event. If you want the best and as much selection as possible, write your lists a few months ahead. And I can't stress this enough: never try out new recipes on the night – always have a dress rehearsal.

# Easter Sunday Lunch serves 8

Easter is the first big celebration for most people after Christmas. It is a big event in our house so we pull out all the stops and have a real party. If you have given up any of your favourite treats, such as chocolate or alcohol, for the past forty days and nights, then Easter Sunday lunch should be a feast eagerly awaited. Of course, you must dye eggs and have an Easter Egg hunt on Sunday morning before settling down to this lunch!

CHAMPAGNE

DEVILLED QUAILS' EGGS ON SPOONS

PRAWN TOASTS

ROAST LEG OF SPRING LAMB

GET-AHEAD ROAST POTATOES

HOME-MADE MINT SAUCE

PURPLE SPROUTING BROCCOLI

CHOCOLATE EASTER EGG MOUSSE WITH SOUR CREAM SAUCE

## devilled quails' eggs on spoons

**16 quails' eggs, hard-boiled**

**8 hens' eggs, hard-boiled, yolks only**

**1 tbsp mayonnaise (home-made is best – see below)**

**1 tbsp Greek yoghurt**

**1 tsp mustard powder**

**salt**

**cayenne pepper**

1 Cut the quails' eggs in half and set aside.

2 Put the hens' hard-boiled egg yolks into a bowl and mash with a fork. Mix in the mayonnaise and yoghurt, mustard powder, salt and a little cayenne pepper until it is smooth.

3 Put each quails' egg half onto a ceramic spoon (or a teaspoon), then spoon the devilled egg yolk onto it, covering the whole yolk. Sprinkle with a little more cayenne pepper and serve with champagne.

## home-made mayonnaise

**300ml sunflower oil (or 100ml olive and 200ml sunflower oil, but don't use too much olive oil or the mayonnaise will taste too bitter)**

**2 egg yolks**

**1½ tbsp lemon juice**

**salt**

**white pepper**

**2–3 tsp Dijon mustard**

1 Pour the oil(s) into a jug. Place a mixing bowl on a damp cloth to stop it spinning while you whisk.

2 Whisk the egg yolks, lemon juice, seasoning and mustard together until light and well blended. When the mix starts to thicken, add the oil in a slow steady stream, whisking constantly – you want to prevent it from curdling so the slower the better. If the mayonnaise is too thin, add more oil; if it is too thick thin it with a little more lemon juice. Taste and adjust seasoning. (This recipe makes 300ml.)

3 If you want to make it in a food processor, use 1 whole egg instead of the 2 egg yolks – it won't be as rich but it is easier and lighter. Continue as above. If it all goes horribly wrong, whisk another egg yolk in a clean bowl and add the curdled mix into it drop by drop.

# prawn toasts

**1kg cooked prawns**

**bay leaf**

**500g soft and flaky fish or whiting fillet**

**ground mace**

**cayenne pepper**

**450g butter at room temperature, plus more for sealing the top of the bowl**

**1** Peel the prawns and put the heads, shells and bay leaf into a pot with just enough cold water to cover them. Set the prawns aside.

**2** Bring the pot up to the boil and simmer rapidly for 15–20 minutes.

**3** Strain the cooking liquor. Discard the heads, shells and bay leaf, and pour the liquor back into the pot.

**4** Add the fish to the pot and cook for about 5 minutes, until flaky.

**5** Transfer the fish to a food processor. Add a pinch of mace and cayenne pepper and process until smooth, adding spoonfuls of the fish liquor to slacken a little and make smooth. You do not want to end up with a slushy mix. Add the butter, then process until completely mixed in.

**6** Roughly chop the prawns and fold them into the processed fish mix, then tip the mix into a bowl. Melt some more butter and pour over the top to seal. (The prawn mixture can be made a day in advance, if you wish.) Spread on toasted bread and serve.

**Aga cooking:** Cook heads and shells as above on the Simmering Plate. Cook the fish as above on the Boiling or Simmering Plate.

# roast leg of spring lamb

**2.5kg leg of spring lamb**

**2 onions, peeled and cut in half**

**4–6 fresh ransoms (wild garlic)**

**8 whole sprigs of fresh rosemary**

**olive oil**

**salt and pepper**

**100ml white wine**

**300ml good stock**

**1** Remove the lamb from the fridge 30 minutes before cooking. Pre-heat the oven to its highest setting

**2** Place the onions cut side down in a heavy roasting tin. Spread out the ransoms and the rosemary sprigs on top, then rest the lamb on them. Rub some olive oil onto the lamb and season with salt and pepper.

**3** Cook the lamb for 20 minutes at the oven's highest temperature, then turn the heat down to 160ºC/325ºF/gas 3 and roast for another 1½ hours or until the meat is done to your liking.

**4** When it is ready, remove the leg of lamb from the oven, transfer to a warm plate and leave to rest for 15 minutes while you make the jus. Remove excess fat from the pan juices.

**5** Put the roasting tin on the hob. Add the white wine and stock and bubble up the pan juices and scrape up any caramelised bits from the bottom.

**6** Check the seasoning. Pour into a warm jug and serve with the lamb. Serve with Get-ahead Roast Potatoes (see page 22).

**Aga cooking:** Slide the tin onto the third or fourth set of runners in the Roasting Oven and cook for 45 minutes, then transfer to the Simmering Oven and roast for another 2–2½ hours or until the meat is done to your liking. Heat the pan juices in the roasting tin on the Simmering or Boiling Plate as above.

# home-made mint sauce

65g butter

6–8 shallots, peeled and chopped

4 tbsp chopped fresh mint

1–1½ tsp caster sugar

salt and pepper

1 Melt the butter in a frying pan over a gentle heat.

2 Add the shallots to the pan and sweat until very soft but not coloured at all. Add the mint, sugar and salt and pepper.

3 Whiz in a food processor until smooth. Keep warm. Serve with the lamb.

**Aga cooking:** Melt the butter on the Simmering Plate.

# purple sprouting broccoli

1kg purple sprouting broccoli, trimmed

olive oil

salt and pepper

1 Bring a pan of water up to the boil. Drop in the broccoli and cook for a few minutes.

2 Drain and tip into an ovenproof dish. Drizzle over a little olive oil – use a fruity one if possible – and season with salt and pepper. Keep warm until ready to serve.

**Aga cooking:** Use the Boiling Plate.

# chocolate easter egg mousse

460g dark chocolate

8 egg whites

200g golden caster sugar

6 egg yolks

100ml double cream

1 Melt the chocolate in a bowl over a saucepan of simmering water.

2 Whisk the egg whites in a very clean bowl, then add the sugar one tablespoon at a time until the mix is very stiff.

3 Stir the egg yolks into the melted chocolate, then add the cream. The mix will become very stiff so stir it well. Fold a good dollop of the whites into the chocolate mix to loosen and stir well to combine. Fold in the whisked egg whites until there are no traces of white and spoon into eight bowls. Cover with clingfilm and refrigerate.

4 Serve with sour cream sauce (see below). (Please note this mousse does contain raw eggs.)

**Aga cooking:** Melt the chocolate at the back of the Aga.

# sour cream sauce

250ml sour cream

250ml whipping cream

1 tsp vanilla extract

caster sugar, to taste

1 Combine the two creams, vanilla extract and sugar to taste.

2 Pour into a serving bowl and pass round with the mousse.

# Foolproof Mothering Sunday Lunch *serves 6*

This menu has been devised to give Mother a day off! Roasting meat on a bed of potatoes is fantastic because it cuts out cooking the veg separately, and for children it is very satisfying and almost magical to be able to produce a delicious lunch all by themselves. Depending on the children's ages, they may or may not need some help from an adult to produce this meal.

> CHICKEN ON A BED OF VEGETABLES
>
> VANILLA ICE CREAM WITH HOT CHOCOLATE SAUCE

## chicken on a bed of vegetables

**2kg organic chicken**

**400g potatoes, peeled and cut into chunks**

**400g carrots, peeled and cut into thick sticks**

**250ml white wine**

**250ml chicken stock**

**4 whole cloves of garlic, unpeeled**

**fresh thyme or rosemary**

**60g butter**

**salt and pepper**

**75ml double cream**

**1** Pre-heat the oven to 200°C/400°F/gas 6.

**2** Put the chicken into a deep, flameproof roasting dish and surround it with the potatoes and carrots. Mix the wine and chicken stock together and pour it over the vegetables. Tuck the garlic cloves and herbs into the vegetables and smear half the butter over the chicken; dot the rest over the vegetables. Season with salt and pepper. Cook for 1 hour or until the juices run clear.

**3** Remove the chicken from the dish and place it on a warmed plate. Remove the garlic cloves and set aside. Using a slotted spoon, spoon the potatoes and carrots around the chicken and set aside to rest. Cover with foil if you wish.

**4** Put the roasting dish on the hob and whisk in the cream over a gentle heat. Squeeze in the softened garlic and whisk again. Reduce for a few minutes.

**5** Check the seasoning. Pour the sauce into a warm jug and serve with the chicken.

**Aga cooking:** Put the dish on the fourth set of runners in the Roasting Oven and cook for 1 hour or until the juices run clear from the chicken. Heat the cream as above on the Simmering Plate.

## vanilla ice cream with hot chocolate sauce

**500g tub of good-quality vanilla ice cream**

**SAUCE:**

**50g good dark chocolate, broken into pieces**

**50g butter**

**125g soft brown sugar**

**2 tbsp cocoa powder**

**200g evaporated milk**

**1 tsp vanilla bean paste**

**1** Melt the chocolate and butter together over a bowl of simmering water or in a microwave. Tip into a saucepan. Beat in the sugar and cocoa powder until smooth. Slowly pour in the evaporated milk, stirring all the time. Add the vanilla bean paste and stir.

**2** Bring the sauce to the boil, then turn down to a simmer and continue to cook for 1 minute.

**3** Remove from the heat and set aside. To re-heat, gently bring up to a simmer. Serve with the ice cream.

**Aga cooking:** Cook as above on the Boiling and Simmering Plates.

*chicken on a bed of vegetables*

# Summer Bank Holiday Drinks Party _serves 12_

A lot of people loathe drinks parties but I think they are the staple of entertaining – it is one way of entertaining a lot of people at once so make it as enjoyable for yourself as possible. I love the fact that I can breeze in and out of conversations and fly about the room, but for my husband, a drinks party is his idea of hell. A great tip is always have a bottle in your hand so you never get stuck with one person for too long. I do think a series of smaller drinks parties are more bearable than one with 100 guests or more, and I would not hesitate to hire a caterer for a big event.

YELLOWFIN TUNA MARINATED IN LIME AND SOY SAUCE

BAKED CAMEMBERT WITH RADISHES

HUMMUS DIP WITH BABY CARROTS

PARMESAN POPCORN

MINI CARAMELISED ONION TARTLETS

WATERMELON, FETA AND BLACK OLIVE CANAPÉS

## yellowfin tuna marinated in lime and soy sauce

**500g fresh yellowfin tuna fillet**

**MARINADE:**

**4 tbsp light olive oil**

**1 tsp sesame oil**

**juice of 3 limes**

**zest of 1 lime**

**1 tbsp Sake or dry sherry**

**1 tbsp soy sauce**

**1 tbsp honey**

**1 red bird's eye chilli, seeds removed, sliced very thinly**

**3cm freshly grated ginger**

**2 spring onions, trimmed and sliced thinly**

**TO SERVE:**

**1 avocado**

**1 tsp sesame seeds**

**3–4 little gem lettuces, washed and spun until dry**

**1 spring onion, trimmed and thinly sliced**

**squeeze of wasabi**

**1** To make the marinade, simply put all the ingredients into a bowl and stir until the honey and salt have dissolved. Taste it at this point for the sweet-to-sour ratio.

**2** Cut the tuna into small cubes and place in the marinade. Cover and let the mixture stand for a minimum of 6 hours or overnight in the refrigerator.

**3** When you are ready to serve, peel the avocado, cut into cubes of a similar size to the tuna and mix into the tuna.

**4** Toast the sesame seeds in a dry frying pan.

**5** Spoon the marinated tuna into the lettuce leaves and sprinkle over some sesame seeds and a few slices of spring onion. Squeeze a dash of wasabi over the top and arrange the lettuce 'cups' on a serving platter. Alternatively, serve the tuna mix on a bed of finely shredded lettuce on individual Chinese ceramic spoons.

_mini caramelised onion tartlets, watermelon, feta and black olive canapés, and yellowfin tuna marinated in lime and soy sauce_

# baked camembert with radishes

1 round Camembert in a wooden box

2 bunches of long radishes, stalks intact

**1** Pre-heat the oven to 180°C/350°F/gas 4.

**2** Remove the cheese from the wrapping and place it in a round ovenproof dish just big enough to hold it. Cook for 15–20 minutes.

**3** Return the cheese back to its box, place in a shallow basket and surround with the radishes. You could also serve this with baby carrots, cucumber sticks and celery.

**Aga cooking:** Place the dish on a baking tray and slide onto the fourth set of runners in the Roasting Oven for 5 minutes, then move to the Simmering Oven and bake for a further 15 minutes or until the cheese has melted and is only just being kept in by its rind. You could bake it entirely in the Roasting Oven but you may have to slide in the cold plain shelf. It will take about 15 minutes but you will have to watch it.

# hummus dip with baby carrots

1 can organic chickpeas in water (240g drained weight), drained but with some of the water reserved

2–3 huge cloves of garlic, peeled

2 tbsp smooth peanut butter

juice and zest of 1 organic lemon

salt and pepper

3–4 tbsp olive oil – choose a mild, fruity oil

1 tbsp toasted pine nuts, to garnish

baby carrots, to serve

**1** Put everything except the oil and the pine nuts into a food processor and whiz until smooth. If it is a bit thick, add some of the reserved chickpea water. Slowly pour in the oil through the feeder at the top until it is the consistency you like.

**2** Drizzle some more olive oil into the bottom of a glass bowl. Spoon in the hummus and scatter over the pine nuts and add a slick of olive oil.

**3** Serve with baby carrots with their stalks still intact.

# parmesan popcorn

1 tbsp sunflower oil

50g whole dried kernels of popcorn

25g butter

1 tbsp chopped fresh rosemary

salt, to taste

150g very finely grated Parmesan (the tubs I normally would tell you not to touch with a barge pole are perfect for this!)

**1** Heat up the sunflower oil in a large saucepan with a lid. Use a high setting on the hob, then turn the heat down.

**2** When it is hot, pour in the corn and shake the pan like mad. When the popping sound stops it is finished. Remove it from the heat and set aside.

**3** To make the topping, melt the butter in a large pan over a gentle heat. Add the rosemary and salt and cook for about 1 minute to release all the flavours. Tip the popcorn into a large bowl and fold in the Parmesan and the flavoured butter, making sure every kernel is coated. Serve straight away.

**Aga cooking:** Use the Simmering or Boiling Plate for the corn. Use the Simmering Plate for the topping.

# mini caramelised onion tartlets

**PASTRY:**

**75g plain flour**

**50g chickpea flour**

**50g unsalted butter, at room temperature and chopped into pieces**

**25g Parmesan cheese, grated, plus extra to serve**

**1 tsp freshly chopped rosemary, plus 3 whole sprigs of rosemary about 10cm long**

**black pepper**

**1 large egg**

**CARAMELISED ONIONS:**

**sunflower oil**

**2 red onions, peeled and thinly sliced**

**1 tbsp soft brown sugar**

**40g unsalted butter**

**1½ tbsp balsamic vinegar**

**salt and pepper**

**1 tbsp freshly chopped rosemary**

**1** To make the pastry, put the flours and butter into the food processor and pulse until the mixture resembles coarse breadcrumbs. Add the cheese, chopped rosemary and pepper and pulse for a couple of seconds until it resembles fine breadcrumbs. Add the egg and pulse again for a few seconds or until soft dough is formed. Flatten the dough into a disc shape, then wrap in clingfilm and refrigerate for at least 30 minutes.

**2** Heat up a little sunflower oil in a frying pan, then toss in the onions, brown sugar, butter and balsamic vinegar. Cook very gently over a medium heat for 10–15 minutes. Season with salt and pepper.

**3** Pre-heat the oven to 200°C/400°F/gas 6.

**4** Brush each hole of a mini muffin tin with some oil. Break the rosemary sprigs into 12 pieces and place them in the bottom of the tin. Spoon the onions over the base of the tin – what you see now will become the tops of the tarts so make them look as good as possible.

**5** Remove the pastry from the fridge and roll out. Using a cookie cutter, cut out sufficient circles to fit over the onion mix in the muffin tin. Carefully lay the pastry circles over the onions, tucking the pastry in around the inside of the holes.

**6** Cook for 10–15 minutes or until the pastry is golden and cooked. Allow to cool in the tin for about 5 minutes.

**7** Place a flat plate or board over the tin and, protecting your hands, invert the tin and give it a gentle shake. Remove the muffin tin and you'll have the little onion tarts staring back at you. If some of the onion gets stuck, ease it off the bottom of the tin with a spoon and slot it back into place. Shave over some Parmesan, drizzle with good balsamic vinegar and arrange on a serving platter.

**Aga cooking:** Place the pan on the floor of the Roasting Oven and cook until the onions are caramelised and thick. Put the tin on the fourth set of runners in the Roasting Oven. Bake the tarts for 10–12 minutes or until the pastry is puffed up and golden. If the pastry browns too quickly, slide in the cold plain shelf just above.

# watermelon, feta and black olive canapés

**500g watermelon (you will have to buy a whole one and cut it up)**

**250g feta cheese**

**400g Greek olives, pitted**

**1** Remove the pips from the watermelon and cut it into bite-sized cubes. Cut the feta cheese into bite-sized cubes. Drain the olives.

**2** Thread an olive, a cube of feta and a cube of watermelon onto a wooden toothpick. Arrange on a plate and serve.

# Bonfire Night Party serves 6

My favourite time of the year is the autumn so I relish the thought of a harvest supper, Halloween and, of course, Guy Fawkes Night. The crisp air and smell of a bonfire are so evocative to me. It is also the ideal time to entertain friends with families – just make sure all the animals are kept safely indoors and keep a close eye on young children. I like to put bales of straw around the bonfire (but not too near), covered with picnic blankets so that the prickles are kept under control, for people to sit on.

> PUMPKIN AND
> COCONUT CURRY
> FIRE CRACKER
> CHERRY CLUSTERS
> CARAMEL POPCORN

## pumpkin and coconut curry

1 tsp coriander seeds

½ tsp ground turmeric

1 tbsp garam masala

1 tbsp clarified butter (see page 158)

2 onions, peeled and chopped

salt

3 cloves of garlic, peeled and crushed

3cm piece of ginger, peeled and grated

1 red chilli, seeded and finely sliced

1.5kg pumpkin, peeled and chopped into 3cm chunks

400ml tin coconut milk

1 heaped tbsp mango chutney

1 large bunch of fresh coriander, roughly chopped

125g desiccated coconut

1 Pre-heat the oven to 180ºC/350ºF/gas 4.

2 Dry fry the spices in a frying pan, then pound them to a powder in a pestle and mortar.

3 Melt the clarified butter in a deep ovenproof pan. Add the onion, cover and cook until soft. Add the spices, salt, garlic, ginger and chilli and cook for 1 minute to release the flavours. Add the pumpkin pieces and coconut milk and bring to a rapid simmer.

4 Cook uncovered for 20–25 minutes or until the pumpkin is tender. Remove from the oven and stir in the chutney. Put the pan back over a medium heat and reduce for 2–3 minutes.

5 Take the pan off the heat, add the chopped coriander and check the seasoning. Scatter over the desiccated coconut. Serve with pilaff rice, yoghurt and diced cucumber.

**Aga cooking:** Cook uncovered in the Simmering Oven for 20–25 minutes or until the pumpkin is tender. Stir in the chutney. Bring it back to the Simmering Plate and reduce for 2–3 minutes.

*pumpkin and coconut curry*

# fire cracker cherry clusters

40g sultanas

80g flaked almonds

140g desiccated coconut

200ml condensed milk

200g dark chocolate chips

180g crushed cornflakes

15 glacé cherries, halved

**1** Pre-heat the oven to 160°C/325°F/gas 3. Line a shallow baking tray with Bake-O-Glide.

**2** Combine everything except the cherries in a bowl and mix well. Drop tablespoons of the mix onto the baking tray. Place the cherry halves into the centre and press down slightly.

**3** Bake in the oven for 10–15 minutes.

**4** Cool slightly on the baking tray, then transfer to a wire rack. Store in an airtight tin.

**Aga cooking:** Bake in the Roasting Oven for 5 minutes.


# caramel popcorn

1 tbsp sunflower oil

75g whole dried kernels of popcorn

180g unsalted butter

420g soft brown sugar

pinch of salt

2 tbsp golden syrup

1 tsp baking soda

85g sliced almonds

**1** Pre-heat the oven to 150°C/300°F/gas 2. Line a shallow baking tray with Bake-O-Glide.

**2** Heat up the sunflower oil in a large lidded saucepan. When it is hot, pour in the popcorn and shake the pan like mad. When the popping sound stops, it is finished. Remove it from the heat and set aside.

**3** Melt the butter over a gentle heat in a large saucepan. Stir in the sugar, salt and golden syrup until the sugar has dissolved and it is all well blended. Bring to the boil and stir for about 2 minutes until it is caramel in colour. Stir in the baking soda. Add the almonds and popcorn, handfuls at a time, making sure all the popcorn is well coated.

**4** Spread out the popcorn mix on the lined baking tray and bake for 40–45 minutes, stirring occasionally.

**5** Remove from the oven and cool completely. Break up and serve.

**Aga cooking:** Cook the popcorn as above on the Boiling Plate. Slide the baking tray into the Simmering Oven and bake for 40–45 minutes, stirring occasionally.

# Christmas Drinks Party *serves 12*

We have friends who throw a big drinks party on Boxing Day every year and Christmas just wouldn't be the same without it. In the USA a lot of people throw open-house parties which usually serve more substantial food than nibbles. These can go on all day rather than for just a few hours, but they are good fun and a great way of entertaining a large number of people.

## mulled wine

I have a much-prized Victorian silver kettle – they used to use them to keep water hot to top up the pot for afternoon tea. Sadly I don't use it very much for hot water these days so I have given it a new job – to keep mulled wine warm, and it looks so pretty on a table.

Mulled wine is usually made with red wine but you can use white as well. I also put a little brandy or port in mine. The quantities can all be adjusted to suit your taste.

Make a spice bag with muslin and put in 1–2 sticks of cinnamon, some cloves, lemon peel, and orange peel. Heat two bottles of wine and a glass of port or brandy in a saucepan with the spice bag, but do not let it boil. Let the spices infuse for a few minutes. Strain and pour into heatproof glasses.

## chicken and rice balls

500g chicken breasts, minced

1 tbsp sunflower oil

1 egg, beaten

1 small onion, peeled and minced

1 red chilli, deseeded and very finely chopped

zest of 2 limes

2 tbsp freshly chopped coriander

salt and pepper

140g basmati rice, cooked

lettuce leaves

DIPPING SAUCE:

90ml soy sauce

30ml fresh lime juice

1 tbsp honey

**1** Mix the minced chicken, oil, egg, onion, chilli, lime zest, coriander, salt and pepper together in a large bowl. Roll into 24 little balls.

**2** Put the cooked rice onto a large plate and roll each ball in the rice. Refrigerate for at least 3 hours or more.

**3** When you are ready to cook the balls, pre-heat the oven to 200°C/400°F/gas 6. Place the balls on a shallow baking tray lined with Bake-O-Glide and cook for 18 minutes.

**4** To make the dipping sauce, simply whisk the three ingredients together and tip into a bowl.

**Aga cooking:** Slide the baking tray onto the third set of runners in the Roasting Oven and cook for 15–20 minutes.

# sweet and spicy nuts

50g butter

1 tbsp freshly chopped rosemary

pinch of dried chilli flakes, or
more if you like it really hot

1 tbsp caster sugar

salt to taste

250g mixed nuts

1 Melt the butter in a large saucepan over a gentle heat. Add the chopped rosemary, chilli flakes, sugar and salt and cook for about 1 minute to release all the flavours.

2 Add the nuts to the saucepan, folding them into the flavoured butter and making sure each one is coated. Drain on kitchen paper. Eat straight away. (You can also use a mixture of seeds, such as pumpkin, flax or sunflower seeds.)

**Aga cooking:** Cook the flavoured butter on the Simmering Plate.

# artichoke melts

1 clove of garlic, peeled

2 anchovy fillets, plus oil from
the tin

1 egg

juice of 1 lemon

175ml olive oil

2 x 250g tins of artichoke hearts
in olive oil

2 tbsp mayonnaise (see page 121)

120g Parmesan cheese, grated

2 packs of ciabatta crispbreads,
toasted

1 To make the marinade, put the garlic, anchovies, their oil, an egg and the juice of a lemon into a food processor and blitz. Pour in the olive oil in a steady stream.

2 Cut the artichoke hearts into quarters, tip into a bowl and pour over the marinade. Leave to marinate overnight.

3 To assemble the canapés, mix the mayonnaise and Parmesan together in a bowl. Spread the toasted ciabatta with some of the mayonnaise mix. Place an artichoke quarter on top and spoon over a little more mayonnaise mix. Repeat until all the artichokes and breads are used up. Place them on to a shallow baking tray.

4 Pre-heat the grill to its highest setting and grill for 2–3 minutes or until they start to brown. Serve warm.

**Aga cooking:** Slide the baking tray onto the first set of runners in the Roasting Oven and 'grill' for 2–3 minutes or until they start to go brown on top. Serve warm.

*goujons of pheasant with aioli, chicken and rice balls,*
*and artichoke melts*

# mini croustades with quails' egg or mushroom filling

**CROUSTADES**

**1 loaf of organic bread, thinly sliced and crusts removed**

**3–4 tbsp melted butter or olive oil**

**QUAILS' EGG FILLING:**

**36 quails' eggs, softly boiled (about 2 minutes)**

**2–3 jars of hollandaise (or home-made, see page 82)**

**MUSHROOM FILLING:**

**3 shallots, peeled and very finely chopped**

**olive oil**

**500g mix of wild mushrooms, very finely chopped**

**1 clove of garlic, peeled and crushed**

**1 tbsp freshly chopped rosemary**

**knob of butter**

**salt and pepper**

**200g goat's cheese**

**1** Pre-heat the oven to 180ºC/350ºF/gas 4.

**2** To make the croustades, use a rolling pin to roll out each slice of bread. Cut into four squares and brush with the butter or oil. Press one square of bread into each mini muffin slot until all the holes are lined. Bake for 6–8 minutes or until golden brown. (One standard loaf will make about 72 croustades. They can be made a day in advance or frozen.)

**3** Remove from the tins and cool. Fill with your choice of filling.

**4** For the quails' egg filling, put an egg into each croustade and spoon over a little hollandaise sauce. Arrange on a platter and serve.

**5** For the mushroom filling, cook the shallots in a little oil until soft. Add the mushrooms and cook for a few minutes, then add the garlic, rosemary, butter, salt and pepper. Continue cooking until the mushrooms are soft. Check the seasoning and set aside to cool (you can refrigerate until required). Put a teaspoon of the mushroom mix into each croustade and crumble over a little goat's cheese. If you wish, warm them through in a hot oven for 2–3 minutes before serving.

**Aga cooking:** Bake the croustades in the Roasting Oven for 5–8 minutes or until golden brown. Cook the mushroom filling on the Simmering Plate. To warm the filled croustades, place in the Simmering Oven for 2–3 minutes.

# goujons of pheasant with aioli

**6–8 pheasant breasts, skinned**

**2 tbsp flour**

**salt and pepper**

**1 organic egg, beaten**

**dry breadcrumbs made from ciabatta or other rustic bread**

**sunflower oil, for frying**

**AIOLI:**

**1 head of garlic**

**150ml olive oil, plus a drizzle for the garlic**

**2 eggs**

**1 tsp Dijon mustard**

**pinch of golden caster sugar**

**salt and pepper**

**1 tbsp white wine vinegar**

**750ml sunflower oil**

**squeeze of lemon juice**

**1 tbsp Greek yoghurt, optional**

**1** Pre-heat the oven to 180°C/350°F/gas 4.

**2** Place the whole head of garlic on a piece of foil large enough to wrap it in and pour over a little olive oil. Wrap it up tightly and bake for about 20 minutes or until it is soft.

**3** Remove the garlic from the oven and let it cool until you are able to handle it. Squeeze out the flesh and mash it in a bowl and set aside.

**4** To make the aioli (garlic mayonnaise), put the eggs, mustard, sugar, salt, pepper and vinegar into a food processor and whiz together. While it is still running, very slowly add the olive and sunflower oils in a steady stream until the mixture is very thick and all the oil has been used.

**5** Switch off the machine and add the cooled roasted garlic and a squeeze of lemon juice. Blend again very quickly just to combine, then taste for seasoning. When you are ready to serve, you can stir in the Greek yoghurt, if using. (The mayonnaise can be kept in the fridge for up to 2 weeks in a covered jar.)

**6** Cut the pheasant breasts into long, finger-like strips. Place the flour, salt and pepper onto a plate and mix together. Put the egg onto a separate plate and breadcrumbs onto another plate.

**7** Dip each strip of pheasant into the seasoned flour, then the egg, then finally coat it well in the breadcrumbs.

**8** Heat enough oil in a frying pan so that the goujons will be totally submerged. The oil is hot enough when a breadcrumb dropped into it sizzles. If you have a deep-fat fryer, this will be ideal.

**9** Fry the goujons a few at a time until crisp and golden. Drain on kitchen paper and season with salt. Keep warm until all the goujons are ready, then serve with garlic mayonnaise.

**Aga cooking:** Bake the garlic head in the Roasting Oven, as above. Fry the goujons on the Boiling Plate.

# gravadlax with sweet dill sauce on rye bread

1½ tbsp golden caster sugar

2½ tbsp coarse sea salt, plus more

freshly ground pepper

1kg salmon tail, cut into two pieces so you have a top and a bottom; it should be filleted but not skinned, all pin bones removed

Dijon mustard

2 tbsp vodka

2 large bunches of fresh dill, finely chopped

loaf of rye bread, sliced thinly

SWEET MUSTARD SAUCE:

4 tbsp Dijon mustard

2 tbsp soft brown muscovado sugar

1½ tbsp white wine vinegar

2 tbsp finely chopped fresh dill

5–6 tbsp sunflower oil

salt and pepper

1 Mix the sugar, salt and pepper together in a bowl. Line a dish big enough to hold the salmon with enough greaseproof paper to wrap the fish up. Lay one half of the salmon skin side down in a shallow glass or china dish.

2 Spread mustard over each piece of salmon and pat half of the salt-sugar mix into it. Spoon over the vodka. Scatter the dill over evenly. Place the second fillet on top of the first, skin side up. Wrap tightly in the greaseproof paper and place a weighted board on top. Chill for 36 hours, turning at regular intervals.

3 To make the sauce, stir the mustard and sugar together. Whisk in the vinegar and dill and then slowly pour in the oil, whisking constantly. Taste for seasoning.

4 When you are ready to serve, scrape half the curing mixture off the salmon. Slice it thinly. Spread a little of the sauce onto the rye bread and top with a slice of gravadlax. Garnish with dill sprigs.

# Christmas Day Lunch serves 8

'Push the boat out and stop moaning!' Those are my words of advice for Christmas – it comes but once a year and the fuss some people make is ridiculous. Just have fun with it. The trick is to start your planning early and do as much preparation as you can the day before, even to the point of setting the table. Here I've given a choice of either goose or turkey for the main course. See page 22 for 'get ahead' roast potatoes. The trifle is a great pudding because it's really just an assembly job and almost all the ingredients can be bought at a good supermarket or deli.

## orange salad with pomegranate seeds and coriander dressing

**6 oranges (preferably blood oranges)**

**2–3 chicory heads – pull the leaves apart and use the smaller leaves**

**1 small red onion, peeled and very thinly sliced**

**2 ripe pomegranates**

**50g pistachio nuts, shelled, peeled to reveal the bright green colour and roughly chopped**

**pitta bread, to serve**

**DRESSING:**

**1–2 tbsp of leftover juice from the oranges**

**4–6 coriander seeds, toasted and ground using a pestle and mortar to make a good pinch of ground coriander**

**1 tbsp white wine vinegar**

**3 tbsp sunflower oil**

**½ tbsp orange blossom water**

**salt**

**1 tsp sugar**

**1** First, segment the oranges. Using a very sharp knife, cut the peel and the pith away from the flesh. Hold the orange over a bowl to catch the juices and carefully dissect out each segment, leaving behind the membrane and skin. Repeat all the way around the orange, squeezing out any juice from the pithy remains. Set the segments aside, leaving them in their juices until you make the dressing. This can be done one day in advance.

**2** To make the dressing, put all the ingredients into a bowl and whisk together or into a screw-top jar and shake vigorously. Taste for seasoning and set aside. This can be made in advance and stored in the fridge.

**3** Put the orange segments, chicory and sliced onion into a bowl and spoon in 3 tablespoons of the dressing, making sure each segment, leaf and onion slice is coated with the dressing. Arrange either on individual plates or on one large platter.

**4** Slice the pomegranates in half and holding them cut side down over the plates or platter, tap the top with a wooden spoon. The seeds should fall out, looking like little jewels on top of the orange salad. Scatter over the pistachios and put any leftover dressing in a jug and hand round with the salad. Serve with slices of toasted pitta bread.

# roast goose

2.5-3kg goose (or buy 2 smaller ones), with giblets and gizzard

1 orange, cut into quarters

salt

STOCK:

neck from the goose

4–6 peppercorns

½ an onion, peeled

1 bay leaf

GRAVY:

glass of port

**1** To make the stock, put the goose neck into a saucepan of cold water with a few peppercorns, the onion and a bay leaf. Bring it up to the boil, then cover with a lid and simmer for 20–25 minutes. Strain and set aside. You will need really good rich stock for the gravy.

**2** Pre-heat the oven to 200°C/400°F/gas 6. Put the goose into a roasting tin. Stuff the cavity with the orange quarters and rub salt all over the bird really well. Pour 500ml of water into the bottom of the tin.

**3** Cook the goose for 40 minutes, then turn the temperature down to 160°C/325°F/gas 3 and continue cooking for 1½–2 hours. You need the meat to be almost falling away from the bones and really crispy skin. Pour off all the goose fat and reserve for roasting potatoes in.

**4** When the goose has finished cooking, remove it from the oven and allow to rest for 5–10 minutes. Keep warm.

**5** It is hard to make the gravy in the pan as there is usually so much fat, but if there are any pan juices deglaze the pan with some red wine and whisk well. Add this to the goose stock made earlier and a glass of port. Reduce the gravy by half and check the seasoning. Serve with chestnut and apple stuffing (see below), apple sauce and roast potatoes (see page 22).

**Aga cooking:** Bring the stock to the boil on the Boiling Plate, then move to the Simmering Oven for an hour or so. To cook the goose, slide the tin on the third set of runners in the Roasting Oven and cook for 1 hour, then transfer to the Simmering Oven for a further 1–2 hours or until the goose is cooked and the skin is really crispy.

# chestnut and apple stuffing

butter, for greasing

4–6 rashers streaky bacon, snipped into pieces

1 large onion, peeled and chopped

600kg chestnuts, either fresh or vacuum-packed, chopped

100g soft prunes, chopped

2 large cooking apples, peeled and chopped

2 heaped tbsp freshly chopped parsley

80g fresh brown breadcrumbs (you may need more depending how dry the breadcrumbs are)

1 egg, beaten

salt and pepper

**1** Pre-heat the oven to 190°C/375°F/gas 5. Grease an ovenproof dish with the butter.

**2** Fry the bacon in a frying pan until crisp, then remove and drain on paper. Fry the onion in the same pan until almost soft, then add the chopped chestnuts, prunes and apple and cook for a further 5 minutes.

**3** Remove from heat, mix in the rest of the ingredients, and bind with the egg. Season with salt and pepper and spoon into the buttered dish. Cook for 25–35 minutes.

**Aga cooking:** Cook the bacon, onion as above on the Simmering or Boiling Plates. Cook the stuffing in the Roasting oven for 20–25 minutes.

# roast turkey

3.5–4.5kg turkey, if possible a Norfolk Bronze (remove the gizzard and use for stock)

1 onion, peeled, cut in half and inserted into the turkey cavity

a good handful of herbs (such as sage, bay or other large leaf herbs), left whole

4 tbsp unsalted butter

salt and pepper

**1** Pre-heat the oven as hot as you can.

**2** Gently loosen the breast skin away from the meat with your fingers, taking great care not to tear the skin. Carefully lifting the skin, arrange the herb leaves underneath the skin in a pretty pattern. Then refrigerate until ready to cook. (This can be done the day before.)

**3** When you are ready to cook, melt the butter and keep it near the oven with a pastry brush so that you are ready to 'paint' the breast with the melted butter. Season well and put the turkey into a deep roasting tin.

**4** Cook the turkey at the highest temperature for 15 minutes, then turn down the heat to 180°C/350°F/gas 4 and continue to cook for about 1½ hours, basting with the butter every 15 minutes or so. Check the turkey breasts after 1½ hours to see if the turkey is cooked – insert a skewer and if the juices run clear it is done, if not put it back into the oven for another 15 minutes and check again. The legs will need the full 1½ hours – check to see whether they are cooked by inserting the skewer as before. If at any point the skin starts to burn, cover with a piece of foil.

**5** Let the turkey rest for at least 20 minutes before carving. Make your gravy and serve with cranberry, redcurrant and walnut stuffing (see below) and roast potatoes (see page 22).

**Aga cooking:** Slide onto the fourth set of runners in the Roasting Oven. Roast for 2–2½ hours, basting with the butter every 15 minutes or so. Check the turkey breasts after 1½ hours to see how cooked it is – it is done when the juices in the thigh meat run clear. If at any point the skin starts to burn, cover with a piece of foil.

# cranberry, redcurrant and walnut stuffing

1 tbsp sunflower oil or goose fat

2 medium onions, peeled and chopped

1.5kg fresh cranberries

225ml redcurrant jelly

splash of Cointreau

250g sourdough breadcrumbs

zest of 2 oranges

180g chopped walnuts

130g soft butter, plus 25g butter, diced

salt and pepper

**1** Pre-heat the oven to 180°C/350°F/gas 4. Butter an ovenproof dish.

**2** Heat the oil or goose fat in a frying pan over a gentle heat. Add the onions and sweat until soft. Add the cranberries and redcurrant jelly and cook until they start to burst. Add the Cointreau and continue to cook for 5–7 minutes until it starts to reduce. Mix in the breadcrumbs, orange zest, and walnuts and 130g butter. Season with salt and pepper. Pile the stuffing into the buttered dish and dot with the diced butter.

**3** Cook for 25–35 minutes or until piping hot. (The stuffing can be made the day before.)

**Aga cooking:** Cook the onions on the Boiling or Simmering Plates, as above. Cook the stuffing in the Roasting Oven, as above.

# pan-fried brussels sprouts with shallots

**150g pancetta cubes**

**butter**

**700g Brussels sprouts, trimmed and cut in half**

**½ tsp chopped thyme leaves**

**125ml double cream**

**salt and pepper**

**1** Fry the pancetta cubes in a frying pan until crispy and remove with a slotted spoon.

**2** Remove any really burnt bits from the pan. If you need a little butter, add some now. Heat the pan so that it is very hot.

**3** Add the Brussels sprouts and thyme to the pan, season with salt and pepper, toss in the pancetta. Add the cream and bubble for a few minutes to reduce a little.

**4** Spoon into a warmed dish and keep warm until ready to serve.

**Aga cooking:** Cook as above on the Boiling or Simmering Plates.


# banoffee trifle

**200g sponge cake (bought or made)**

**100ml Tia Maria or espresso**

**300ml double cream**

**250ml custard (bought or made)**

**450g jar of dulche de leche (cooked condensed milk, found in the gourmet section of supermarkets)**

**4–5 ripe bananas**

**PRALINE:**

**170g granulated sugar**

**100g sliced blanched almonds**

**1** Line a baking tray with Bake-O-Glide or baking parchment and set aside.

**2** To make the praline, pour the sugar and 2 tablespoons of water into a heavy-bottomed saucepan. Cook over a low heat until the sugar has dissolved. Turn the heat up to medium and cook until the sugar turns amber in colour.

**3** Quickly stir in the almonds and pour onto the prepared baking tray. Spread out evenly and leave to cool. When cooled, break into small pieces.

**4** Break the sponge cake into pieces and line a glass serving bowl. Spoon over the Tia Maria or espresso so the sponge cake is thoroughly soaked.

**5** Whip the cream to the soft peak stage – it should fall into gentle folds and just hold. Fold half the whipped cream into the custard. Pour the dulche de leche over the sponge cake, then slice the bananas and scatter over. Spoon the custard cream mix on top of that, then finish with a layer of pure whipped cream. Scatter over the praline shards and serve.

**Aga cooking:** Cook the praline on the Simmering and Boiling Plates.

# Boxing Day Tea *serves 8*

Boxing Day tea is the perfect time to entertain friends. In our house we serve it by the fire and everyone is so cosy and comfortable that they linger over it for hours. I must say the satisfaction level is high as everyone is so grateful that all they have to do is take what is offered and not have to move to a table.

COLD SAUSAGE
SANDWICHES

SAVOURY RICOTTA STRUDEL

MINCEMEAT CAKE WITH
BRANDY BUTTER ICING

## cold sausage sandwiches

**12 good-quality pork sausages**
**honey**
**8 medium slices of bread**
**butter**
**chilli jam or mustard**

**1** Pre-heat the oven to 190°C/375°F/gas 5. Line a shallow baking tray with Bake-O-Glide.

**2** Brush the sausages with some honey (do not prick them), then put them onto the baking tray. Cook for 15–20 minutes. You want them to be sticky and slightly charred.

**3** Remove the sausages from the oven, split them lengthways and leave to cool.

**4** Toast the bread. Cut off one end of the bread and carefully slide a knife in to ease open the centre of the bread, taking care not to tear the whole piece open – you want to create a pocket. Spread the inside with soft butter and the chilli jam or mustard, keeping the pocket intact. Tuck three sausage halves inside and serve.

**Aga cooking:** Cook the sausages in the Roasting Oven for 15 minutes. Toast the bread using the Aga toasting rack.

# savoury ricotta strudel

olive oil

2 large onions, peeled and finely chopped

zest and juice of 1½ lemons

100g breadcrumbs

1 tbsp raisins

1 tbsp freshly chopped sage

2 tbsp pine nuts, toasted and chopped, plus 1 tbsp toasted and left whole

1 jar of roasted peppers in olive oil, drained (reserve the oil)

1 tbsp rice flour

650kg ricotta cheese

4 eggs

60g Parmesan cheese, grated

4–6 fresh sage leaves, torn

salt and pepper

190g ready-made filo pastry

flour

100g butter, melted

1 Heat some olive oil in a large frying pan and fry the chopped onions until soft. Using a slotted spoon, transfer them to a large bowl and let them cool to room temperature. Do not wash the frying pan.

2 Using the same frying pan, add the juice and zest of the lemons and cook until the juice evaporates. Add the breadcrumbs and fry until golden, then add the raisins, sage, 1 tablespoon of the soft onions and all the pine nuts. Stir well, then tip onto a plate lined with kitchen paper and set aside. (This can be done the day before.)

3 The next day or when the onions are cool, take the bowl of cooked onions and add the drained peppers, rice flour, ricotta, eggs, Parmesan and torn sage leaves. Season with salt and pepper and mix well.

4 Soak a tea towel in water and wring it out well. You will need this to keep the filo pastry damp while you work. Cover the filo pastry with it to keep it soft and pliable.

5 Pre-heat the oven to 180°C/350°F/gas 4. Line a large shallow baking tray with Bake-O-Glide.

6 Spread out another tea towel and sprinkle it with flour. Lay two sheets of filo onto this and brush with melted butter. Lay another sheet of filo on top and butter it, then repeat with another layer.

7 Scatter the breadcrumb mixture on one end of the pastry, then spoon half the ricotta filling on top of the breadcrumbs. Lay two more sheets of filo over this and brush with butter, then spoon the rest of the ricotta mix over the pastry at the same end, so you end up with a sandwich of pastry, breadcrumbs, filling, pastry and filling.

8 Using the tea towel to guide you, roll up the pastry as you would for a Swiss Roll. Carefully transfer the roll to the prepared baking tray and brush with more butter. Tuck the edges in neatly. Bake for 25–30 minutes until golden brown.

9 Dust with Parmesan cheese. Leave to cool and slice as required.

Aga cooking: Cook the onions and breadcrumbs on the Simmering Plate. Bake on the fourth set of runners in the Roasting Oven with the cold plain shelf above for 30–40 minutes until golden brown. For 4-oven Aga cookers, bake in the Baking Oven.

*savoury ricotta strudel*

# mincemeat cake with brandy butter icing

**CAKE:**

**150g mincemeat**

**275g self-raising flour**

**225g golden caster sugar**

**225g unsalted butter, softened, or baking margarine**

**2 tsp baking powder**

**1 tsp vanilla extract**

**5 eggs**

**ICING:**

**125g golden icing sugar, sifted**

**250g soft unsalted butter, cubed**

**4–6 tbsp brandy**

**1** Pre-heat the oven to 180°C/350°F/gas 4. Line either a shallow traybake tin with Bake-O-Glide or two round 20cm cake tins (not too deep).

**2** Put all the cake ingredients into the bowl of an electric mixer and mix until well combined (you can also do this by hand). Pour the batter into the prepared tin and smooth over the top with a palette knife.

**3** Bake the small cakes for 35–40 minutes or the large traybake cake for 40–45 minutes. The cake is done when it springs back when lightly pressed in the middle and it pulls away from the sides of the tin.

**4** Remove the cake from the oven and cool in the tin on a wire rack.

**5** To make the icing, beat the icing sugar into the butter and stir in the brandy little by little, keeping the mixture stiffish and not too thin.

**6** When the cake is cool, spread over the brandy butter icing.

**Aga cooking:** Bake on the fourth set of runners in the Roasting Oven with the cold plain shelf on the second set of runners for 20–25 minutes. For 4-oven Aga cookers, bake in the Baking Oven.

# New Year's Day Brunch serves 6

Because we still have young children and it is impossible to find a baby-sitter on New Year's Eve, we have a dinner party at home. It is great fun and we do eat and drink very well. I think 11:30am is the perfect time to serve brunch on New Year's Day as no one feels pressurised into getting up early after a late night. Start off with a glass of champagne or a pick-me-up, then linger over the rest of the brunch.

CHAMPAGNE

HERB WATER

PICK-ME-UP

BIRCHER MUESLI

POACHED EGGS WITH
CHEAT'S HOLLANDAISE

SMOKED SALMON AND
POTATO PIZZETA

## herb water

**6 mint sprigs**

**juice of 1 lemon**

**3cm fresh ginger, cut into strips**

**1** Put all the ingredients into a jug and top up with chilled mineral water.

## pick-me-up

**220ml strong green tea, cooled**

**220ml pineapple juice**

**180g fresh pineapple, chopped**

**2 tbsp soy powder**

**1–2 tsp honey**

**1 banana**

**ice**

**1** Blend all the ingredients in a blender until puréed and serve. (To get the most out of this, the ingredients should be organic.)

## bircher muesli

**HOME-MADE MUESLI:**

**400g porridge oats**

**175g bran**

**180g toasted mixed nuts
(such as almonds, walnuts
and hazelnuts)**

**200g chopped mixed dried
organic fruit (such as figs,
apricots, apples and dates)**

**TO SERVE:**

**natural yoghurt**

**mixed berries (such as Alpine
strawberries, raspberries and
blackberries)**

**1 tbsp brown sugar**

**grated apple**

**honey, to taste**

**1** To make the muesli, simply mix the all ingredients together and store in an airtight tin. (You could also use a good-quality store-bought muesli.)
**2** To serve, mix the muesli, yoghurt, berries, sugar and grated apple together and spoon into glass bowls. Serve with more fresh fruit and honey.

# smoked salmon and potato pizzeta

3 large potatoes, peeled and very finely sliced (you will need a mandolin)

75–80g clarified butter (see page 158)

salt and pepper

crème fraîche

500g smoked salmon

**1** Soak the sliced potatoes in iced water for 10 minutes, then drain and pat as dry as possible.

**2** Heat up the clarified butter in a frying pan.

**3** When the butter is sizzling, arrange the potato slices in a circle in the frying pan, overlapping the slices, until they are all used up. You only want one layer. Season with salt and pepper.

**4** Cook the potatoes over a medium heat for 8–10 minutes. Flip the potato pizzeta over and continue to cook for another 8-10 minutes or until the potatoes are tender and golden on both sides.

**5** Slide the pizzeta onto a plate, spread over the crème fraîche and top with the salmon.

**Aga cooking:** Heat the clarified butter on the Boiling Plate, then continue on the Boiling or Simmering Plates or the Roasting Oven floor.

# poached eggs with cheat's hollandaise

3 English muffins, split, or 6 slices of brioche

6 eggs – must be very fresh

6 slices of good ham or smoked salmon (optional)

butter

CHEAT'S HOLLANDAISE:

6 egg yolks

salt and pepper

1 tbsp lemon juice

250g unsalted butter, melted

**1** To make the hollandaise, process the egg yolks, salt, pepper, and lemon juice in a food processor. Pour the melted butter into the food processor while it is still running in a steady stream. Taste for seasoning. Use straight away. You can add some freshly chopped herbs if you wish – fold them in at the end.

**2** Poach the eggs (see page 81) or re-heat. (You can poach eggs the day before – keep them in a bowl of cold water in the fridge and re-heat them by plunging them into boiling water just before serving.)

**3** Toast the brioche or muffins and butter them. Slide on the egg and coat in the hollandaise. You can add ham or smoked salmon if you wish – just top the brioche or muffin with a slice of either, top with the egg and continue. Serve straight away.

**Aga cooking:** Toast the brioche or muffins using the Aga toasting rack.

*poached eggs with cheat's hollandaise*

# white tie, top hat and tails

Although almost every magazine and book seems to have 'easy' in the title, there is no getting away from the fact that to entertain on a formal level will be more time consuming and not that simple. However, it can be easier with helpful advice, but when you do push the boat out, expect more work and preparation.

As long as you know this, you are now armed with the knowledge that you will have to put aside more time and perhaps get a little more help. While most of our entertaining is informal, I relish all the pomp and ceremony that go with formal dinners and lunches. I start well in advance: I arrange the flowers two days beforehand and put them in a cool, draught-free area; I polish the silver a week before and wrap it well so that it stays in tip-top shape. It is amazing what a fantastic high you get when your guests look at your table and acknowledge all the hard work you have put into it. That is what makes it all worthwhile to me; it is like applause to an actor.

**tips**

● Plan your evening down to the last detail. Work out a timetable/working plan that includes everything from taking into account your bath to cooking times. Make a list of all the advance cooking you can do and get on with it.

● Make sure you are ready half an hour before guests are due to arrive. I know this sounds obvious but it's not always easy to achieve.

● Set the table early, the day before if possible.

● Make sure at least one of the dishes in your menu can be served cold or can be prepared completely in advance.

● Always wear an apron in the kitchen!

# Charity Lunch serves 6

I truly believe a committee of one is best as that is often the quickest way to make decisions, but unfortunately very few events are run on that basis. The object of a charity function is to raise money. Just as much work, time and effort go into raising £5 as they do in raising £50,000, so you might as well aim high and delegate jobs to those who won't let you down. Dare to be different – just because a lunch with a speaker worked for the last umpteen years doesn't mean you can't try something different. However, do bear in mind that nine times out of ten the money is to be made by the over-forties and that people in their fifties and sixties will come to more daytime events, while the young will attend balls and dinners. The recipes I've given here are easy to prepare for large numbers. For the Autumn/Winter menu, try asking a local shoot to donate pheasants – this is a good money-maker as it means the main course will cost you almost nothing!

SPRING/SUMMER LUNCH

CHICKEN AND PEACH SALAD WITH LEMON POPPY SEED DRESSING

OR

MANGO CHICKEN SALAD

HERBED RICE SALAD

SOFT FRUIT TARTS WITH LEMON CURD


AUTUMN/WINTER LUNCH

PHEASANT NORMANDY

OR

POUSSINS WITH MARSALA AND THYME

MASHED POTATO

POACHED PEARS WITH GINGER CREAM

## Spring/Summer

## chicken and peach salad with lemon poppy seed dressing

**800g cooked chicken breasts, skinned and cut into chunks**

**6 ripe peaches, peeled, stoned and cut into slices**

**1 tbsp freshly snipped chives**

**rocket, to serve**

**DRESSING:**

**juice and zest of 1 lemon**

**1 tbsp poppy seeds**

**2 tbsp sour cream**

**1 tbsp olive oil**

**2 tbsp sunflower oil**

**1 tsp honey**

**salt and pepper**

**1** Mix the lemon juice, zest, poppy seeds, sour cream, oils, honey, salt and pepper together in a big bowl. Check the seasoning.

**2** Fold in the chicken pieces, peaches and chives. Serve with a rocket salad.

# mango chicken salad

800g cooked chicken breasts, skinned and cut into chunks

1 large ripe mango, peeled and diced

1 tbsp freshly chopped tarragon

rocket and watercress, to serve

**DRESSING:**

200g thick Greek yoghurt

4 tbsp mayonnaise (see page 121)

juice and zest of 1 lime or more to taste (or use the juice of 1 lemon and half the zest)

3 tbsp mango chutney

1 tbsp garam masala

½ tsp smoked paprika

salt

**1** Mix the yoghurt, mayonnaise, lime juice, zest, chutney, garam masala and paprika together and season with salt.

**2** Fold in the chicken pieces, mango and tarragon. Serve with a rocket and watercress salad.

# herbed rice salad

1 small onion, peeled and finely chopped

butter and sunflower oil

235g rice

400ml stock or water

1 tsp salt

**HERB DRESSING:**

1 tbsp freshly chopped tarragon

1 tbsp freshly chopped flat leaf parsley

½ tbsp freshly chopped mint

1 tbsp tarragon vinegar

3 tbsp mild olive oil

salt and pepper

pinch of sugar

**1** Fry the onion in a little butter and oil until soft, then add the rice, stirring well to coat every grain with the oil/butter. Pour in the stock or water and season with salt.

**2** Bring up to the boil, then turn the heat down and simmer for about 15–20 minutes or until the water is absorbed. (Brown rice will take 30–40 minutes.)

**3** To make the dressing, whisk all the ingredients together. Pour the dressing over the cooked rice, leave to cool and serve with the chicken salads.

**Aga cooking:** Cook the onion on the Simmering Plate. Put the rice, water and salt into a large saucepan and bring it up to the boil on the Boiling Plate. Stir it once, then cover with a lid and put it on the Simmering Oven floor for 15–20 minutes. Remove it from the oven, take off the lid and fluff up with a fork. Cover the pan with a clean tea towel to absorb some of the steam.

*soft fruit tarts with lemon curd*

## soft fruit tarts with lemon curd

**POLENTA PASTRY:**

**300g plain flour**

**120g golden caster sugar**

**pinch of salt**

**180g unsalted butter, cold and cubed**

**80g polenta**

**2 whole eggs, beaten**

**1 egg yolk, beaten, for egg wash**

**FILLING:**

**300g good-quality lemon curd**

**600g soft fruit, such as blueberries and raspberries**

**1 tbsp icing sugar**

**1** To make the pastry, sift the flour, sugar and salt into a food processor, then add the butter and polenta and process for 30 seconds. Add the two whole eggs and process again until it forms a ball (you may have to add a little cold water, 1 tablespoon at a time, if the mixture is dry). Stop immediately, wrap the pastry in clingfilm and let it rest in the fridge for a minimum of 30 minutes.

**2** Pre-heat the oven to 170ºC/340ºF/gas 3½.

**3** When the pastry has rested, roll out and line a 20.5cm loose-based tart tin. Lay a piece of greaseproof paper over it, fill with baking beans, and blind-bake for 10 minutes. Remove from the oven and take out the beans. Brush on a little egg wash and return to the oven floor for another 5 minutes or until the pastry is done. Cool completely on a wire rack.

**4** When the pastry case has cooled, remove it from the tin and spread the lemon curd over the base. Scatter the fruit over and dust with icing sugar. Chill in the fridge for 30 minutes or more and serve with crème fraîche.

**Aga cooking:** Brush on the egg wash and cook the pastry case in the Roasting Oven for 10 minutes or until the pastry is done.

# Autumn/Winter:

## pheasant normandy

3 large pheasants, jointed

2–4 tbsp clarified butter (see page 158)

150g cubed pancetta or smoked bacon

2 onions, peeled and roughly chopped

8 juniper berries, crushed

pinch of cloves

salt and pepper

3 apples, peeled, cored and sliced

200ml Calvados

300–500ml game or chicken stock

2 tbsp crème fraîche

1 Pre-heat the oven to 170ºC/340ºF/gas 3½.

2 In a large flameproof casserole, brown the pheasant joints in the clarified butter, then remove them to a plate.

3 Put the pancetta and onions into the casserole and cook until lightly browned. Add the juniper berries, cloves, salt and pepper and the pheasant joints, layering the apple slices in between. Pour in the Calvados and enough stock to cover and bring to the boil, then reduce to a simmer for 10 minutes. Transfer the casserole to the oven and cook for 1–1½ hours.

4 When you are ready to serve, swirl in the crème fraîche and serve with mashed potatoes. (This casserole tastes even better if made the day before and reheated.)

**Aga cooking:** Brown the pheasant on the Simmering Plate. Cook the casserole in the Roasting Oven for 20 minutes, then transfer to the Simmering Oven for 1–2 hours.

## poussins with marsala and thyme

6 poussins (or partridge)

6–8 tbsp clarified butter (see page 158)

2 red onions, peeled and roughly chopped

8 sprigs of thyme

4 sprigs of rosemary

300ml Marsala

650ml chicken stock

salt and pepper

150ml double cream

1 Pre-heat the oven to 190ºC/375ºF/gas 5.

2 Brown the poussins in the clarified butter in a large casserole or deep roasting tin, then remove them to a plate. Add the onions to the tin and cook until lightly browned. Add the herbs and place the poussins on top. Finally, add the Marsala, stock and salt and pepper and bring to the boil. Cook in the oven for 35–40 minutes or until the poussins are done.

3 When you are ready to serve, remove the poussins to a warmed plate. Scrape up all the crusty bits at the bottom of the casserole or tin and pour in the cream. Reduce for 2 minutes over a gentle heat, then serve with the poussins.

4 Serve with large croûtons on the side (see page 171). Croûtons can be made a week in advance and kept in an airtight container.

**Aga cooking:** Brown the poussins and onions on the Simmering and Boiling Plates. Cook in the Roasting Oven for 35–40 minutes. Reduce the sauce on the Simmering Plate.

*pheasant normandy*

# clarified butter

To make clarified butter, put the butter in a saucepan over a low heat. When the butter has melted, drain off all the clear yellow liquid, leaving behind the white solids. You only need the clear yellow liquid, so discard the rest. Store in a jar in the fridge.

**Aga cooking:** Leave the butter at the back of the Aga.

# poached pears with ginger cream

**110g golden caster sugar**

**5cm piece of ginger, peeled and cut into strips**

**6 firm pears, peeled with stems intact**

**250ml double cream**

**2–3 pieces of crystallised ginger, finely chopped, and syrup from the jar**

**1** Place the sugar and ginger in a large saucepan with 1 litre of water. Bring up to the boil and stir until all the sugar dissolves.

**2** Place the pears into the boiling liquid and simmer for 18–20 minutes or until they are tender.

**3** Remove the pan from the heat and cool the pears in the liquid, turning the pears from time to time.

**4** Using a slotted spoon, transfer the pears to a dish. Sieve the poaching liquor into a clean saucepan. Bring back to the boil, turn the heat down and reduce until syrupy. Pour the syrup over the pears and set aside to cool.

**5** When you are ready to serve, whip the cream to soft peaks and fold into the chopped crystallised ginger. Place a pear in each bowl and spoon over some crystallised ginger syrup and cream.

**Aga cooking:** Cook the sugar and ginger on the Boiling Plate as above. Add the pears and cook in the Simmering Oven for 20–40 minutes or until tender. Reduce the syrup on the Simmering Plate.

# Summer Buffet before the Ball

**serves 8**

I live on the Isle of Wight where summer means beaches, boats and Cowes Week, and Cowes Week equals balls. There is one held every night during Cowes Week. I have done my fair share of buffets before the ball and, believe me, it is hard work. The cooking is the easy part – it's the clearing up that is a pain. If possible, hire some staff so that when you return home in the wee small hours, the house is back to normal. Nothing is better than coming home and having 'breakfast' at 3am. That's when the real fun starts as party post-mortems are my absolute favourite thing in the world. You can make the kedgeree in advance and ask the help who did all the clearing up to lay the table for your early hours feast.

CRAB-STUFFED
TOMATOES

COLD ROAST BEEF
WITH CRÈME FRAÎCHE
HORSERADISH

GREEN SALAD

NEW POTATOES WITH
CAVIAR

SCARLET TART

CHOCOLATE CREAM
POTS

AFTER THE BALL

KEDGEREE

## crab-stuffed tomatoes

8 large firm, slightly under-ripe beefsteak tomatoes

olive oil

salt and pepper

3–4 tbsp home-made mayonnaise (see page 121) or store-bought

Tabasco sauce, to taste

½ tbsp Worcestershire sauce

1 tbsp tomato ketchup

1 tbsp brandy

juice of 1 lemon

700g white crab meat, picked over (or you could use prawns)

2 tbsp finely chopped fresh tarragon

1 Cut off the tops of the tomatoes about halfway down from the stem end and carefully scoop out the seeds. Reserve the lids. Try not to break or split the tomatoes. Brush the insides of the tomatoes with a little olive oil and season with a little salt and pepper.

2 Mix the mayonnaise, Tabasco, Worcestershire sauce, ketchup, brandy and lemon juice together and season with salt and pepper. Taste and adjust the seasoning as necessary.

3 Fold the crab meat and tarragon into the sauce, then stuff each tomato with the crab mix. Put the lid on, cover with clingfilm and chill for an hour before serving.

# cold roast beef with crème fraîche horseradish

2 tbsp dripping or oil
900g fillet of beef

HORSERADISH SAUCE:
2–4 tbsp prepared horseradish
200ml crème fraîche
1 tsp white wine vinegar
salt and pepper
a little sugar, to taste (optional)

**1** Pre-heat the oven to 200°C/400°F/gas 6.

**2** Put the dripping or oil into a roasting tin and put onto a direct heat. When the fat is smoking, seal the meat on all sides (there is nothing more to sealing meat than simply browning it quickly). Take care as the fat will spit. Drain off any excess fat.

**3** Cook the beef for 15–20 minutes (depending on the size of the fillet) but no longer than this. When the cooking time is up, take the fillet out of the oven and remove from the tin.

**4** Wrap the meat very, very tightly in good-quality clingfilm, twisting the ends for a really snug fit. Put the fillet onto a plate and leave it to rest for at least 20 minutes. To serve the meat, remove the clingfilm and carve.

**5** To make the sauce, simply stir all the ingredients together and season to taste. Serve with a green salad.

**Aga cooking:** Seal the meat as above on the Boiling Plate. Cook the beef in the Roasting Oven as above.

# new potatoes with caviar

750g new potatoes, as small as possible
dry white wine, enough to cover the potatoes
juice of ½ a lemon
salt and pepper
3 tbsp olive oil
caviar – as much as you can afford
200ml sour cream

**1** Place the potatoes into a large pot of salted water and bring to the boil. When the potatoes are cooked (about 15 minutes), drain them and tip them into a bowl.

**2** Pour over enough white wine to cover the potatoes and marinate them for about 20 minutes.

**3** Meanwhile, make the vinaigrette by whisking the lemon juice, salt, pepper and olive oil together and set aside.

**4** Drain the potatoes and dress them with the vinaigrette. Just before serving them, gently fold in the caviar and top with the sour cream.

**Aga cooking:** Cook the potatoes on the Boiling Plate, or use the Simmering Oven method (see pages 22–3).

*new potatoes with caviar*

# scarlet tart

**75g unsalted butter**

**250g sweet oat biscuits, crushed with a rolling pin**

**FILLING:**

**500g mascarpone cheese**

**3 very fresh organic egg yolks**

**120g icing sugar**

**500g strawberries, hulled and cut into quarters.**

**1** Melt the butter in a saucepan and mix into the crushed biscuits. Press the biscuit mix into a 25-cm loose-bottomed tart tin. Chill in the fridge until set.

**2** Make the filling. Beat the mascarpone until fluffy. In a separate bowl, beat the eggs and sugar, then fold into the mascarpone.

**3** Spread the mascarpone mix over the biscuit base and top with the strawberries. Chill and serve. (Please note that the filling contains raw egg.)

# chocolate cream pots

**150g chocolate, chopped**

**340ml double cream**

**340ml milk**

**1 whole split vanilla pod**

**4 tbsp caster sugar**

**8 egg yolks**

**1** Melt the chocolate and the cream together in a saucepan over a gentle heat. Pour the milk into a pan, scrape the vanilla pod seeds into the milk and add the sugar. Gently bring to a simmer.

**2** In another bowl, whisk together the egg yolks. Take the milk off the heat and add to the egg yolks little by little, whisking constantly, until it is all in. Pour in the chocolate cream mixture and stir.

**3** Tip the mixture back into the pan and stir over a gentle heat until it coats the back of a wooden spoon.

**4** Strain into individual ramekins and cool, then cover with clingfilm and refrigerate. Serve with an amaretti biscuit.

**Aga cooking:** Melt the chocolate and cream very gently as above on the Simmering Plate or in the Simmering Oven. Heat the egg yolk mixture as above on the Simmering Plate.

# After the Ball

## kedgeree

600g smoked haddock, all bones removed

450g basmati rice

1 tbsp sunflower oil

1 large onion, peeled and chopped

30g clarified butter (see page 158)

1½ tsp garam masala

1 apple, peeled, cored and finely diced

½ tsp turmeric

1 tbsp sultanas, plumped up with boiling water

2 tbsp freshly chopped flat leaf parsley (or watercress)

200ml double cream (optional – if you like your kedgeree creamy)

6 hard-boiled eggs, peeled and cut into quarters

1 Lay the fish in a large roasting tin on the hob and pour over enough water to cover – about 1 litre. Bring the water up to a rapid simmer and cook for 5–10 minutes, but do not over-cook the fish.

2 Remove the fish from the water and reserve the cooking liquid. Skin and flake the fish into large pieces. Keep it warm.

3 Put the rice into a saucepan with a lid and pour in the reserved cooking water – if it needs a little more water, add some but I use just under double the amount of water to rice ratio. Bring the rice to a boil, then cook for 15–20 minutes or until the rice is ready.

4 Heat the sunflower oil in a large frying pan, add the chopped onion and fry for 5–8 minutes until the onion is soft and starting to char around the edges.

5 In the same frying pan, melt the clarified butter and add the garam masala, apple and turmeric. Stir for a few minutes, then remove from the heat.

6 Add the cooked rice to the onion mix, then add the fish, sultanas, and parsley. If using cream, pour it in now. Season to taste (you probably won't need to add salt) and mix gently with a fork, trying not to break up the flakes of fish. Transfer the kedgeree to a warmed serving dish. Top with the hard-boiled eggs, sprinkle over a little more parsley and serve. (Alternatively, the fish, rice and onion mix can all be cooked separately in advance. When you are ready to eat, warm everything through and mix together.)

Aga cooking: Cook the fish as above on the Simmering Plate. Put the rice into a saucepan and add the reserved cooking water. Bring to the boil on the Boiling Plate, cover with a lid and transfer to the floor of the Simmering Oven for 20 minutes. Cook the onion on the floor of the Roasting Oven, as above.

lunches, teas and kitchen suppers

We often have people over for kitchen suppers midweek. It's an ideal time for an impromptu get-together and it releases you from the obligation to produce dinner-party food and extravagant table settings. In fact, I wouldn't be surprised to discover that most people do the bulk of their entertaining this way.

## weekday lunch

Weekday lunches are difficult for most people as they are at work, but if you can organise one, they are huge fun. It is a time when you can cook different types of food, especially if you host a women-only lunch as generally they prefer lighter dishes. Lunch is also an opportunity to entertain elderly friends who may find it difficult to drive at night.

## afternoon tea

Wouldn't it be nice to bring back the rituals of a proper tea every day? In our house, tea is a big feature during the shooting season and in the summer months. When the weather is good, we sometimes take a thermos of tea, sandwiches and cake down to the beach – even in winter – which is pure bliss. Somehow it doesn't seem to matter if there is sand in the sandwiches. And if I want to give my family a real treat, nothing beats honeycomb-and-butter sandwiches – always a winner.

## tips

- Don't always eat in the kitchen – look for cosy spots around your house and create a fabulous and different atmosphere. Try supper and a game of scrabble around the fire.
- For informal lunches or suppers, try cooking outside over some hot coals or a brazier, even in the winter.
- One or two brilliant cheeses are better than a mediocre pudding and they make the perfect ending to lunch or supper.
- Look for silver-plated hot water jugs in antique shops and markets – when your teapot needs refilling, you won't need to return to the kitchen.

# More Tea, Vicar? *serves 6*

So few people stop for tea these days. If they do, it is literally a cup of tea and a biscuit, so when the opportunity arises, a proper afternoon tea is a fantastic way to entertain. It feels a bit like going to the cinema in the middle of the day – a real treat!

CREAMED KIPPERS ON TOAST

HOT BUTTERED TEA CAKES

WALNUT AND COFFEE SPONGE CAKE

DROP SCONES

## creamed kippers on toast

400g flaked kipper, all bones removed

100g unsalted butter, softened

pepper

140g cream cheese

4 tbsp double cream

1 anchovy

pinch caster sugar

juice of ½–1 small organic lemon, to taste

clarified butter (see page 158)

1 Put the kipper, unsalted butter, pepper, cream cheese, double cream, anchovy, sugar, and lemon zest into the bowl of a food processor and blitz until smooth. Check the consistency – you want a smooth pâté, not too loose or stiff. If it is too stiff, add a little more double cream. Check the seasoning. I like to add lemon juice at the end to taste – this is optional.

2 Pour it into a serving dish and cover with melted clarified butter. Serve with hot buttered toast for tea.

## hot buttered tea cakes

20g fresh yeast

180ml tepid milk

450g plain flour

75g golden caster sugar

pinch of salt

½ tsp allspice

50g butter, softened

50g candied peel

30g sultanas

1 egg, beaten

1 tbsp golden caster sugar mixed with some water, to form a glaze

1 Crumble the yeast into the milk and mix until it is smooth. Put the flour and sugar into the bowl of an electric mixer with the dough hook attached and start the mixer on a slow speed. Pour in the yeast and milk. Add the salt, allspice and butter and knead really well. The dough is ready when it comes away from the sides of the bowl.

2 Put the dough into a large, lightly greased bowl and stand in a warm place for 1–2 hours or until it has doubled in size.

3 Tip the dough out onto a floured surface and scatter over the candied peel and sultanas. Knead the fruit into the dough so that it is evenly distributed.

4 Divide the dough into 8–10 small balls. Line a baking tray with Bake-O-Glide. Put the balls of dough onto the tray and press each one down to flatten. Leave to rise in a warm place for 30 minutes, then glaze with beaten egg.

5 Pre-heat the oven to 200ºC/400ºF/gas 6. Bake the tea cakes in the middle of the oven for 10–15 minutes or until golden.

6 When cooked, remove from the oven and immediately brush each tea cake with the sugar-water glaze. Cool on a wire rack. To serve, cut in half, toast and liberally spread with butter.

**Aga cooking:** Bake on the grid shelf on the third set of runners in the Roasting Oven for 10–15 minutes or until the tea cakes are golden.

# walnut and coffee sponge cake

275g self-raising flour

225g golden caster sugar

225g unsalted butter, softened, or baking margarine

2 tsp baking powder

2 tsp coffee mixed with 1 tbsp boiling water

100g chopped walnuts, plus walnut halves for decorating

5 eggs

ICING:

75g unsalted butter, softened

200g icing sugar

1 tbsp coffee essence

1 Pre-heat the oven to 180°C/350°F/gas 4. Line two 20.5cm sponge tins with Bake-O-Glide.

2 Put all the cake ingredients into the bowl of an electric mixer and mix until well combined. Divide the cake mix between the prepared cake tins.

3 Bake for 30–35 minutes. The cakes are ready when gently coming away from the sides of the tin and spring back when lightly pressed on top.

4 Stand the cakes in their tins on a wire rack for a minute, then remove them from the tins and cool on the rack.

5 To make the icing, beat all the ingredients together until smooth. Spread half of the icing over one sponge cake and sandwich with the other. Spread the remaining icing on the top and decorate with walnut halves.

Aga cooking: Place the grid shelf on the floor of the Roasting Oven and place the cake tins to the right on the grid shelf. Slide the cold plain shelf onto the third set of runners and bake the cakes for 20 minutes or until they are golden on top, gently coming away from the sides and spring back when lightly pressed on top.

# drop scones

100g self-raising flour

120ml buttermilk

30g golden caster sugar

1 large organic egg

a little oil, for greasing

1 Put all the ingredients except the oil into a bowl and mix really well with a whisk, so there are no lumps.

2 Cook the scones in batches. Heat a little oil in a shallow frying pan, flat baking stone or line a frying pan with Bake-O-Glide. Using a tablespoon, drop the mix onto the hot surface and cook until it starts to bubble, then flip the scone over and cook for 1 minute or until golden.

3 Serve with butter and honeycomb. This quantity makes approximately 15 scones.

Aga cooking: Place a piece of Bake-O-Glide on the Simmering Plate and grease with a little oil, spoon on the batter and cook as above.

*walnut and coffee sponge cake*

# Harvest Supper _serves 6_

My year always starts in September, with the beginning of the new school year, so to kick it off I like to have a good old-fashioned harvest supper. Historically, this was to give thanks for the harvest and reward the farm workers for all their hard work over the summer months. Now it is a good excuse to invite lots of friends round and catch up after the summer holidays!

MULLED CIDER

SQUASH AND APPLE SOUP

POT-ROASTED SAUSAGES WITH GRAPES

BAKED SWEET POTATOES

PAN-FRIED GREEN CABBAGE

ROASTED PLUMS AND QUINCES

## mulled cider

**2 litres medium-dry cider**

**3 cinnamon sticks**

**2 apples, studded with clove**

**½ tsp allspice**

**30ml rum**

**sugar, to taste (optional)**

**cinnamon swizzle sticks, to serve**

**1** Combine all the ingredients except the swizzle sticks in a large saucepan. Simmer over a low heat for 20 minutes.

**2** Serve hot with a cinnamon swizzle stick. This quantity serves 12–15.

**Aga cooking:** Simmer on the Simmering Plate for 20 minutes.

# squash and apple soup

1.5kg butternut squash

6 tbsp olive oil

salt and pepper

1 onion, peeled and chopped

1 parsnip, peeled and chopped

2 apples, peeled, cored and chopped

3cm piece of fresh ginger, grated, or more to taste

good grating of nutmeg

750ml good-quality chicken or vegetable stock

2 tbsp double cream

3 slices of bread

2–3 tbsp clarified butter (see page 158)

6 dried organic apple rings, to serve

**1** Pre-heat the oven to 190ºC/375ºF/gas 5.

**2** Cut the butternut squash in half. Remove the seeds and any fibre, then slice the halves into quarters. Place on a baking tray. Brush each quarter with a tablespoon of olive oil and sprinkle over some salt and pepper. Roast for about 20–25 minutes until soft and slightly charred around the edges.

**3** Set the squash aside to cool, then scrape away the flesh from the skin and reserve.

**4** While the squash is cooking, heat the remaining oil in a deep pan. Add the onion and cook gently until soft. Add the parsnip, apple, ginger and nutmeg and cook for 3–5 minutes. Pour in the stock and bring to the boil. Turn down the heat and simmer for 20–25 minutes or until the parsnips are tender.

**5** Meanwhile, make the croûtons. Pre-heat the oven to 170ºC/340ºF/gas 3½. Cut the bread into cubes and toss in a bowl with the clarified butter, making sure they are well coated. Spread onto a baking tray. Bake for 8–10 minutes or until golden. Watch them carefully as they burn very easily. Leave to cool on a plate lined with kitchen paper.

**6** When the squash is ready, tip it into the pan with the onions and parsnip and check the seasoning, adding salt and pepper as needed. Use a food processor to purée the soup, return it to the pan, add the cream and warm through. Serve with the croûtons and a dried apple ring.

**Aga cooking:** Roast the squash in the Roasting Oven for 15–20 minutes. Cook the onion and parsnip as above on the Boiling or Simmering Plate, then add the stock and simmer in the Simmering Oven for 10–15 minutes or until the parsnips are tender. Bake the croûtons in the Roasting Oven for 8 minutes or until golden.

## pot-roasted sausages with grapes

**1.5kg black seedless grapes**
**slick of good-quality olive oil**
**18 good-quality sausages**
**500ml red wine**
**2–3 sprigs of fresh thyme**
**salt and pepper**

**1** Pre-heat the oven to 160°C/325°F/gas 3.

**2** Pick the grapes from the bunches and wash. Using a potato masher, crush the grapes well, or pulse in a food processor.

**3** You will need a flameproof, heavy-based casserole with a tightly fitting lid. Heat up a little olive oil in the casserole and gently brown the sausages. Pour over the crushed grapes, wine, and the thyme sprigs and season. Bring to the boil, put the lid on and cook in the oven for 1–1½ hours, then remove the lid and cook for another 20–30 minutes to reduce the juices.

**4** Serve with boiled new potatoes or baked sweet potatoes (see below) and pan-fried green cabbage (see page 174).

**Aga cooking:** Brown the sausages in the casserole on the Simmering Plate. Add the crushed grapes, wine and thyme. Cook, covered, in the Roasting Oven for 20 minutes. Remove the lid and transfer to the Simmering Oven for 1–1½ hours.

## baked sweet potatoes

**1 sweet potato per person, washed (not too big as they are quite rich)**
**knob of butter**
**salt and pepper**

**1** Pre-heat the oven to 200°/400°F/gas 6.

**2** Wrap each sweet potato in foil. Bake for 45–60 minutes or until the potato is tender.

**3** Remove from the foil and split open. Drop in a knob of butter and season with salt and pepper.

**Aga cooking:** Bake in the Roasting Oven as above, but there is no need to wrap in foil.

*pot-roasted sausages with grapes*

# pan-fried green cabbage

1½ tbsp goose fat

1 tbsp clarified butter
(see page 158)

1 large head of white cabbage,
shredded very finely

salt and pepper

pinch of ground coriander

zest of 1 organic orange

1 You will need a very large pan to fry it all at once or do it in two batches. Heat the goose fat and clarified butter in the pan until very hot. Fry the cabbage, season with salt, pepper and ground coriander, then toss in the orange zest. Turn the heat down if too hot – burnt cabbage is disgusting! Stir and cook for 3–5 minutes.

2 Spoon the cabbage into a warmed dish and serve.

**Aga cooking:** Cook as above on the Boiling and Simmering Plates.


# roasted plums and quinces

3 quinces, peeled, cored and cut
into quarters

55ml organic honey

1 cinnamon stick

12 ripe plums, cut in half and
stones removed

250ml Greek yoghurt

60g pistachio nuts, chopped

1 Pre-heat the oven to 220ºC/425ºF/gas 7.

2 Bring the quinces, 150ml water, honey and cinnamon up to the boil in a saucepan and simmer for 5 minutes (the quinces may need more poaching time if they are very hard).

3 Spread two large pieces of foil over a deep baking tray, forming a cross. The foil must be large enough to hold all the plums and the liquid and be gathered at the top to form an enclosed parcel. Spread the plums onto the foil and pour over the quince liquor. Wrap up the parcel. Bake for 25–30 minutes or until the fruit is soft and tender.

4 Transfer the quinces and plums to a warmed serving dish. Pour the cooking liquor into a saucepan. Reduce the liquor for 3–5 minutes over a gentle heat until it is thick and syrupy (sometimes this is not necessary as it thickens in the foil.)

5 Serve with a dollop of Greek yoghurt and chopped pistachios.

**Aga cooking:** Simmer the quinces as above on the Simmering Plate, then bake in the Roasting Oven as above. Reduce the syrup as above on the Simmering Plate.

# Walking Lunch serves 12

We have some wonderful walks all over the country and to make the most of this, I have held a number of 'walking lunches'. I write the invitation on an out-of-date ordnance survey map and enclose a map with a cross marking the lunch destination – everyone has to make their own way there on foot by a certain time. In the past I have set up tents in friends' fields, laid out a buffet in the back of the car and organised a treasure hunt along the way – all part of the fun. The chilli can easily be made in advance and reheated. Instead of making a dessert, serve crisp apples with chunks of tasty Montgomery cheese, oatcakes and quince paste.

> CHILLI WITH PITTA STRIPS
> AND SOUR CREAM
>
> OATCAKES
>
> APPLES AND MONTGOMERY
> CHEESE WITH QUINCE
> PASTE
>
> HOT SPICED COFFEE WITH
> WHIPPED CREAM

## chilli with pitta strips and sour cream

100ml olive oil

2kg good-quality minced beef

500g chorizo sausage, skin removed and chopped

6–8 red onions, peeled and finely chopped

6–8 cloves of garlic, peeled and crushed

6–8 x 400-g tins of plum tomatoes

6 red peppers, deseeded and chopped into pieces

2 hot chilli peppers, seeds in for added heat (or removed for a milder heat), chopped

cayenne pepper, to taste

½ tsp ground cumin

2 x 400-g tins of organic kidney beans in water, drained

salt and pepper

TO SERVE:

pitta bread, toasted and roughly torn into strips, or tortilla chips

chopped spring onions

sour cream

strong Cheddar cheese, grated

1 Heat up the olive oil in a frying pan and brown the minced meat and chorizo sausage. You may need to do this in batches. It is important not to over-crowd the pan as you want the meat to brown, rather than steam. Transfer the meat to another dish.

2 If you need more oil, add it to the pan, then fry the onions until they are soft but not coloured. Add the garlic, tomatoes, peppers, chilli and spices. Cook for about 1 minute. Tip the meat back in and bring the sauce up to the boil, then simmer for 25–30 minutes. After the 30 minutes, taste for seasoning, then add the beans. Cook for another 20–30 minutes.

3 Serve in large bowls with pitta strips or tortilla chips, chopped spring onions, sour cream and Cheddar cheese.

Aga cooking: Brown the meat as above on the Simmering Plate. Cook the onions and other ingredients on the Simmering Plate. Add the meat, bring the sauce up to the boil on the Boiling Plate and boil for 2–3 minutes, then transfer to the Roasting Oven for 20 minutes. Add the beans and move to the Simmering Oven for another hour or so.

# oatcakes

30g bacon fat or lard

½ tsp bicarbonate of soda

½ tsp salt

450g oatmeal, plus more for dusting and rolling

1 tbsp chilli flakes (optional)

cracked black pepper (optional)

1 Pre-heat the oven to 180°C/350°F/gas 4. Line a shallow baking tray with Bake-O-Glide.

2 Melt the fat with 300ml hot water. Add the bicarbonate of soda and salt to the oatmeal. If you wish to flavour the oatcakes with chilli flakes or black pepper, add them now. Make a well in the oatmeal, then pour in the water. Using a knife, cut the mixture to make a firm dough.

3 Sprinkle the worktop with oatmeal. Roll the dough out thinly and cut out rounds or squares. Place the oatcakes on the tray. Bake for 20 minutes or until dry and crisp. Cool on a wire rack and store in an airtight tin.

**Aga cooking:** Cook on the Roasting Oven floor for 10–15 minutes.

# quince paste

2kg quinces

preserving sugar

1 Wash and buff the quinces to remove any 'fuzz' on the skin. Chop into pieces, put into a large, deep pan and cover with 1 litre of water. Bring the pan to the boil, then simmer for 1–2 hours until the quinces are soft.

2 Sieve the quince mix and measure the pulp. To every 550ml of pulp, add 450g of preserving sugar.

3 Put the quince pulp and sugar into a stainless steel saucepan. Bring to the boil. Stir the mix until it is thick and paste-like. Do not let it stick or burn.

4 When the paste is ready, lay some Bake-O-Glide in a tin or on a flat surface. Pour the quince paste onto the Bake-O-Glide and leave it to cool completely, then chop into small cubes to serve with apples and cheese.

**Aga cooking:** Bring the quinces to the boil on the Boiling Plate, then transfer to the Simmering Oven for 1–2 hours, or until soft. Bring the pulp to the boil on the Boiling Plate. You may have to move the pan between the Boiling and Simmering Plates if the heat is too intense.

# hot spiced coffee with whipped cream

300ml double cream

1 vanilla pod

2 cinnamon sticks

750ml pot of freshly brewed strong coffee

2 tbsp sugar

100ml rum

450ml milk

1 Whip the cream and set aside.

2 Split the vanilla pod and put it into a large saucepan with the cinnamon sticks, the coffee, sugar and rum and bring to a gentle simmer for 2–3 minutes. Remove the cinnamon sticks and vanilla pod. Add the milk and heat so that it almost reaches the boil. Remove from the heat. Pour into large cups and dollop the whipped cream on top. Serve right away. If transporting in a thermos flask, don't add the whipped cream.

**Aga cooking:** Heat as above on the Simmering and Boiling Plates.

# Al Fresco Summer Lunch

serves 6

Who wants to cook in the heat of summer? Certainly not me! I want dishes that can be put together with very little effort, prepared ahead of time and can wait until we are ready to eat. This menu fulfils all these criteria and is perfect for lunch in the garden.

PIEDMONT PEPPERS

ASPARAGUS MOUSSE

CLASSIC CREAMY COLESLAW

CORN-ON-THE-COB WRAPPED IN PANCETTA

GRILLED SUMMER VEGETABLES WITH BAGNA CAUDA

TOASTED BULGUR WHEAT

PROFITEROLES WITH PISTACHIO ICE CREAM AND CARAMEL SAUCE

## piedmont peppers

**6 red, yellow or orange peppers (not green ones)**

**18 cherry tomatoes**

**2 tins of anchovies in olive oil**

**about 30 basil leaves**

**3–4 cloves of garlic, peeled and thinly sliced**

**salt and pepper**

**olive oil**

**1** Pre-heat the oven to 180°C/350°F/gas 4.

**2** Leaving the stalk intact, cut the peppers in half straight through the stalk and remove the seeds and ribs.

**3** Spread the pepper halves on a shallow baking tray. Cut the tomatoes in half and put three halves into each pepper half. Tuck in an anchovy, a couple of basil leaves and a slice or two of garlic. Season with a very little bit of salt and a good grinding of pepper. Drizzle over the oil from the anchovy tins and then continue with olive oil. Roast the peppers for 25–30 minutes.

**4** Serve at room temperature with crusty bread to mop up the juices.

**Aga cooking:** Slide the baking tray onto the second set of runners in the Roasting Oven and bake for 25–35 minutes or until the peppers are soft and tender.

# asparagus mousse

**butter**

**500g asparagus**

**500ml double cream**

**3 organic egg yolks, plus
1 whole egg, beaten**

**salt and pepper**

**lemon juice**

**olive oil**

**1** Pre-heat the oven to 160°C/325°F/gas 3. Line a large roasting tin with a tea towel. Butter six ramekins and place them on the tea towel in the roasting tin. Set aside.

**2** Bring a pot of water up to the boil, add some salt and blanch the asparagus for 2 minutes.

**3** Refresh the asparagus in iced water and drain. Cut off the tips and reserve. Trim off and discard any tough woody ends. Chop the asparagus into small pieces.

**4** Pour 250ml of the cream into a saucepan, add the chopped asparagus. Simmer for a few minutes until the asparagus is really tender.

**5** Blend the cream and asparagus in a food processor or blender, then add the rest of the cream. Stir in the eggs and season with salt and pepper. Strain the mousse mixture into the ramekins, then pour boiling water into the roasting tin to come halfway up the sides of the ramekins.

**6** Carefully slide the tin into the oven and cook until the mousse is set – this will take 30–45 minutes, but check it after 20 minutes.

**7** Serve the mousse with the asparagus tips tossed in a little lemon juice and good olive oil.

**Aga cooking:** Blanch the asparagus as above on the Boiling Plate. Cook the cream as above on the Simmering Plate. Slide the ramekins and roasting tin into the Simmering Oven and cook as above.

# classic creamy coleslaw

500g white cabbage or a mixture of red, green and white

3 large carrots

½ onion, or more to taste (optional)

salt and pepper

2–3 tbsp sour cream

300ml home-made mayonnaise (see page 121)

DRESSING:

1 tbsp white wine vinegar

3 tbsp sunflower oil

1 tsp honey or caster sugar

salt and pepper

1 tsp Dijon mustard

**1** Grate the cabbage, carrots and onion to the same coarseness.

**2** Whisk the dressing ingredients together, then toss the cabbage, carrot and onion in the dressing and leave for 20–30 minutes.

**3** Drain any excess dressing from the cabbage and mix in the sour cream and mayonnaise. Check the seasoning and serve.

# corn-on-the-cob wrapped in pancetta

PER PERSON

1 ear of corn, preferably freshly picked

1 slice of pancetta

olive oil

**1** Pre-heat the oven to 200ºC/400ºF/gas 6.

**2** Pull back the husks from each ear of corn to expose the corn, but do not remove them. Remove the silky threads. Wrap a slice of pancetta around the corn, drizzle with a little olive oil, then rewrap with the husks. Tie the husks at the top with butcher's string if necessary.

**3** Bake the corn on the oven shelf or a baking tray for 20–25 minutes, turning it every so often – it will start to blister and colour but that is good (you may need to pull back the husks towards the end of the cooking time to colour the pancetta). You can also cook the corn on a barbecue or under a conventional grill turned to its highest setting.

**4** Serve with more good-quality olive oil.

**Aga cooking:** Cook on the grid shelf on the Roasting Oven floor.

# grilled summer vegetables with bagna cauda

3 courgettes, sliced

3 fennel, sliced

2 red and 1 yellow peppers, deseeded and thickly sliced

12–15 baby carrots, washed

olive oil

salt and pepper

BAGNA CAUDA:

100g unsalted butter

2 tins of anchovies in olive oil

350–400ml good olive oil, not too strong

salt

5–6 fat cloves of garlic, peeled and crushed

TO SERVE:

500g fresh peas in their pods – try to select small pods

150g bunch of radishes, trimmed but with stalk intact

500g really tiny new potatoes, boiled

1 You will need a large ridged grill pan for this recipe. Put the griddle on to a heat source for at least 10 minutes or until it is smoking hot.

2 While it is heating up, brush the courgette slices, fennel, peppers and carrots with some olive oil. Season them with salt and pepper, then lay them on the griddle and cook until they are charred on both sides and tender but still with a bit of a bite. The courgettes will not take as much time as the other veg. You will have to cook the vegetables in batches, but as this dish is to be served at room temperature, you can do this earlier in the day.

3 You will need a heavy-based saucepan for making the bagna cauda. You want everything to melt and come together slowly with this dish – it is not to be rushed. Melt the butter in the saucepan over a low heat. Add the anchovies and any of the oil from the tins. Cook for 3–5 minutes until it all starts to break down. Add the garlic to the anchovies, stirring all the time. Don't let the garlic burn or colour. Whisking very slowly, dribble in the olive oil. When all of the ingredients are smooth, the sauce is ready.

4 Taste the sauce, then season with salt if necessary. Pour the sauce into a warm bowl. It is meant to be kept hot so you may want to put it on a food warmer or over some votives.

5 Arrange the cooked vegetables on a large platter and add the raw radishes and peas still in their pods and the cooked new potatoes. Serve with the sauce and with rustic breads.

Aga cooking: Cook the vegetables as above on the floor of the Roasting Oven. Cook the bagna cauda as above on the Simmering Plate.

*grilled summer vegetables with bagna cauda*

# toasted bulgur wheat

2 red onions, peeled and thinly sliced

mild olive oil

1 tsp sugar

350g bulgur wheat (preferably coarse)

100g raisins

1 dried chilli, crumbled

½ tsp ground cumin

½ tsp ground coriander

pinch of allspice

3–4 ripe tomatoes, diced very small

juice and zest of 1 lemon

1 bunch of fresh mint, chopped

1 bunch of flat leaf parsley, chopped

150g toasted pine nuts

salt and pepper

**1** This needs to be made at least 3 hours before you want to serve it so that it takes in all the flavours. Pre-heat the oven to 180°C/350°F/gas 4. Line a shallow baking tray with Bake-O-Glide.

**2** Put the sliced onions in a bowl and add 1 tablespoon of olive oil and the sugar. Stir it all together, then spread out the onions on the prepared tray. Cook in the oven for 15–18 minutes, stirring occasionally, or until the onions are soft and caramelised.

**3** Meanwhile, pour the bulgur wheat into a shallow bowl and pour over cold salted water to cover. Leave to soak for 45 minutes or until tender. Drain any excess water away and squeeze out in a sieve.

**4** Put the raisins in a bowl and pour over some boiling water. Let them soak for 10–15 minutes or until plump. Drain and set aside.

**5** When the bulgur wheat, onions and raisins are all ready to use, put them into a large bowl and add the spices, tomatoes, lemon juice and zest and herbs. Stir together, then add the nuts and olive oil to taste. It doesn't want to swim in oil – add it slowly so that everything is only just coated. Season with salt and pepper. Cover with clingfilm and leave in a cool place until you are ready to serve.

**Aga cooking:** Cook the onions in the Roasting Oven as above.

# profiteroles with pistachio ice cream and caramel sauce

**CARAMEL SAUCE:**

**50g butter**

**150g golden syrup**

**75g soft brown sugar**

**50g unrefined granulated sugar**

**100ml double cream**

**½ tsp vanilla bean paste or extract**

**PROFITEROLES:**

**50g butter, cut into pieces**

**60g plain flour, sifted**

**1 tsp golden caster sugar, mixed into the flour**

**2 eggs, beaten**

**TO SERVE:**

**good-quality pistachio ice cream**

**1** The caramel sauce, which can be served hot or cold, can be made 2 days in advance. Melt the butter, golden syrup and both sugars together over a low heat until the sugar has dissolved. Let it bubble gently for a few minutes but do not let it burn. Slowly pour in the double cream, stirring all the time. Add the vanilla bean paste and stir. Bring to the boil, remove from the heat and stir. Set aside. Store in a jar in the fridge if making in advance.

**2** For the profiteroles, line a shallow baking tray with Bake-O-Glide. Run it under a cold tap and shake off the excess water. Pre-heat the oven to 180°C/350°F/gas 4.

**3** Put 150ml cold water and the butter into a saucepan and bring to the boil.

**4** Remove the pan from the heat and quickly add in the flour and sugar, stirring vigorously with a wooden spoon until well combined and the mix comes away from the sides of the pan – this will take a minute or so. Beat in the eggs a little at a time, until thick and glossy (you may not need all the eggs). You should end up with a smooth glossy paste.

**5** Drop teaspoonfuls of the mix onto the prepared tray. This quantity should make about 18 buns. Bake for 15–20 minutes or until the buns are crisp, puffed up and golden.

**6** Split the buns in half horizontally and leave to cool on a wire rack.

**7** When you are ready to serve them, scoop ice cream into the bottom half of each profiterole and cover with the top. Drizzle over the caramel sauce and serve. To get ahead with the serving of this dish, scoop ice cream balls onto a tray lined with greaseproof paper and open-freeze them. When you are ready to assemble, just take out the scoops of ice cream and pop them onto the profiterole bottoms.

**Aga cooking:** Cook the sauce as above on the Simmering Plate. For the profiteroles, heat the water and butter as above on the Boiling Plate. Bake on the second set of runners in the Roasting Oven with the cold plain shelf above for 10–15 minutes.

# Winter Lunch Party serves 6

This is a great menu to serve in the cold winter months when you want a change from casseroles, and it's perfect for an indulgent middle-of-the-week lunch party. When I first came to the UK and had lasagne, I thought it was terrible. I like it the way my mother makes it and she was taught in the 'Old Neighbourhood' in Chicago by her Italian neighbour, so I guess this is the Italian/American version of the traditional dish.

## old neighbourhood lasagne

olive oil

2 onions, finely chopped

3 large tins of good-quality Italian plum tomatoes – about 2 kg

salt and pepper

450g ricotta cheese

100g Parmesan cheese, finely grated, plus 1 tbsp for topping

500g mozzarella cheese grated, plus 2 tbsp for topping

1 egg

freshly grated nutmeg

1 bunch of basil, torn

butter

18–20 sheets of fresh lasagne sheets (from the chilled food section of a deli)

**1** Heat up a tablespoon of olive oil in a heavy-bottomed saucepan and fry the onions until soft. Add the tomatoes and season with salt and pepper. Bring up to the boil, then turn down the heat and simmer uncovered for 30 minutes or until it has reduced to about 1 litre.

**2** Put the cheeses, egg, grating of nutmeg and basil into a bowl. Season with salt and pepper and mix together.

**3** Grease a deep-sided ovenproof dish with some butter. Put a ladleful of the tomato sauce on the bottom of the dish and spread it out. Lay three sheets of pasta on the sauce, overlapping slightly. Pour over some more sauce and scatter with some of the cheese mix. Repeat this until all the lasagne sheets, sauce and the cheese are used up, ending with a layer of pasta. Sprinkle the rest of the cheese over the pasta for the topping. You can freeze this dish at this point or prepare it up to this stage 2 days in advance.

**4** To cook, bring the lasagne back to room temperature. Pre-heat the oven to 180°C/350°F/gas 4. Cook for 30–40 minutes or until it is bubbling and browning.

**5** Serve with lots of garlic bread and a green salad of romaine lettuce.

**Aga cooking:** Cook the tomatoes for 45–60 minutes in the Simmering Oven. Slide the lasagne onto the third set of runners in the Roasting Oven for 25–30 minutes or until it is bubbling and browning.

# garlic bread

**1 whole head of garlic**

**olive oil**

**250g butter**

**salt**

**2 ciabatta loaves (I like to use part-baked ciabatta bread but you can also use a French stick)**

**1** Pre-heat the oven to 180ºC/350ºF/gas 4.

**2** First, roast the garlic. Place the whole head of garlic on a piece of foil large enough to wrap it in and pour over a little olive oil. Wrap it up tightly and roast for 20–25 minutes or until it is soft.

**3** Remove the garlic from the oven and let it cool until you are able to handle it. Squeeze out the flesh, mash it in a bowl and set aside. Add the butter and salt to taste and beat well.

**4** Pre-heat the oven to 180ºC/350ºF/gas 4. Slice the bread on a diagonal but not all the way through, so that the slices are still intact at the bottom. Spread each side of the sliced bread with the butter and garlic mix. Wrap the bread in foil. Bake for 15–18 minutes. Serve hot.

**Aga cooking:** Roast the garlic in the Roasting Oven as above. Bake the bread in the Roasting Oven as above.

# almond cookies

**400g ground almonds**

**150g golden caster sugar**

**2–3 drops of almond extract**

**2 eggs**

**2 tbsp milk**

**golden icing sugar**

**1** Pre-heat the oven to 170ºC/340ºF/gas 3½. Line a baking tray with Bake-O-Glide.

**2** Put the ground almonds and sugar into a food processor. Pulse for a few seconds. Add the almond extract, eggs and 1 tablespoon of milk. Process again, adding the remaining milk slowly – you only just want it to form a soft dough.

**3** Shape the dough into crescent shapes (this quantity will make about 20 cookies). Spread them out on the prepared baking tray. Bake for 10–15 minutes.

**4** Remove the cookies from the oven and cool on a wire rack. Dust them liberally with icing sugar and serve with a glass of Amaretto.

**Aga cooking:** Bake on the third set of runners in the Roasting Oven with the cold plain shelf above for 8–10 minutes. For 4-oven Aga cookers, bake on the third set of runners in the Baking Oven for 8–10 minutes.

# Children's Birthday Tea Party  *serves 6*

With everyone trying to eat more healthily, it is amazing that we still give our children store-bought 'e'-loaded food. My children love a good tea party and to eat home-made crisps is a real treat, as I am as guilty as the next mother of giving my children store-bought food. But when I make them, I really do feel that I am doing my bit to encourage better, if not entirely healthy, eating! Any drink tastes better with a straw in it, and you don't even need to set a table – buy cardboard cake boxes from the local bakery or gather up old shoe boxes. Wrap up all the food and put it in each box along with a carton of juice, napkin and a straw. You can then put each child's name on the box and put them round the table, or wrap them up like parcels and pile them up for the children to find their own box.

---

HOME-MADE CRISPS AND BACON DIP

MARMITE BREAD

CRUMPETS WITH CHOCOLATE JAM

JELLY WHIP

ICE-CREAM FLOATS

CUPCAKE BIRTHDAY CAKE

---

## home-made crisps

**500g Desiree potatoes**
**sunflower oil**
**salt**

**1** Slice the potatoes so they are about the thickness of a crisp, using a mandolin. Soak them in cold water for 10 minutes and drain. Dry them really well.

**2** Use a deep fat fryer if you have one, or a heavy bottomed pan. Heat up the oil – about 5–6cm deep when melted. Test that the oil is hot enough by throwing in a breadcrumb to see if it sizzles. Fry the potato slices in batches.

**3** Drain on kitchen paper and sprinkle with salt. Keep in an airtight bag or tin. Serve with the bacon dip (see page 187).

**Aga cooking:** Fry carefully on the Boiling or Simmering Plate.

## bacon dip

**200g cream cheese**

**1 tbsp mayonnaise**

**1 tbsp double cream**

**1 slice of onion**

**3 rashers of bacon, cooked**

**1** Put all the ingredients into the bowl of a food processor and blitz until super smooth.

**2** Taste for seasoning and serve with the crisps (see page 186).

## marmite bread

**1 packet of ready-to-make bread mix**

**milk – use instead of water in the bread mix**

**3 tbsp Marmite**

**45g butter, softened**

**1** Scald the milk in a saucepan over a gentle heat. Add 2 tablespoons of the Marmite and stir to dissolve.

**2** Make the bread according to the packet instructions, using the Marmite milk instead of the water.

**3** Mix the remaining Marmite with the butter.

**4** Shape the dough into an oblong and spread with Marmite butter. Roll up the dough and put into a 450g loaf tin. Leave to rise. Bake according to the packet instructions. Cool in the tin for 10 minutes and turn out on to a wire rack. Cool completely. Serve with soft boiled eggs.

**Aga cooking:** Scald the milk on the Simmering Plate.

## home-made chocolate jam

**200g dark chocolate, chopped into pieces**

**300g unsalted butter**

**500ml condensed milk**

**70g ground almonds or hazelnuts (optional)**

**1** Put the chocolate and butter in a bowl and melt over a pan of simmering water.

**2** When it has melted, stir well and add the rest of the ingredients. Pour into a sterilised jar and store in the fridge. Spread on crumpets, toast or bread.

**Aga cooking:** Melt on the Simmering Plate.

# jelly whip

tasteless oil, such as grapeseed

580ml gold-top Jersey milk

4 leaves of gelatine

85ml double cream – the best you can buy, but not too thick

150g caster sugar

200g strawberries, puréed with 1 tbsp caster sugar in a food processor and sieved (or bought strawberry purée)

strawberries, to serve

**1** You will need either individual ramekins or a 20.5 cm jelly mould. Lightly grease the bowl with a tasteless oil, such as grapeseed.

**2** Put about 4 tablespoons of the milk into a flat bowl and soak the gelatine leaves so they become very soft.

**3** Put the rest of the milk, cream and sugar into a saucepan and gently heat so that it just reaches a gentle boil.

**4** Remove from the heat and add the soaking gelatine and any of the soaking milk. Strain the mix through a sieve. Fold in the strawberry purée and pour into the jelly mould. Cover with clingfilm and refrigerate overnight.

**5** To serve, dip the base of the mould in hot water and gently squeeze the mould if it is plastic or coax it out with a gentle push of clean fingers. Invert a plate over the top of the mould and shake to release the jelly. Serve with more strawberries.

**Aga cooking:** Heat the milk, cream and sugar on the Simmering Plate.

# ice-cream floats

12 scoops of vanilla ice cream

100ml chocolate sauce (see page 125)

coca cola

**1** Put 2 scoops of ice cream into each tall glass, then add a teaspoon of chocolate sauce and top up with coca cola.

**2** Serve with straws and stand back for the sugar rush!

# cupcake birthday cake

550g self-raising flour

400g caster sugar

450g unsalted butter or margarine

4 tsp baking powder

8 large eggs

6–8 tbsp milk

ICING:

450g icing sugar

6–8 tbsp water or milk

2 packet of small sweets

food colouring (optional)

**1** Pre-heat the oven to 180°C/350°F/gas 4. Line a large 24-hole muffin tin with paper cupcake cases and set aside.

**2** Tip all the cake ingredients into a bowl and mix well until combined (I use a food processor and beat for about 2 minutes). Fill the cupcake cases half full and level off the tops.

**3** Bake for 20 minutes, checking halfway through and turning if necessary. They are done when they spring back when gently pressed on top. Remove the cakes from the tin and cool on a wire rack.

**4** To make the icing, mix the sugar and liquid and beat until smooth. Spoon onto the cakes and top with the sweets. Pile the cakes in a pyramid shape on a large plate. Stick the amount of candles you need in randomly and put a sparkler in the top cupcake.

**Aga cooking:** Put the muffin tin into a roasting tin and slide the tin onto the third or fourth set of runners in the Roasting Oven. Bake for 15–20 minutes.

*ice-cream floats*

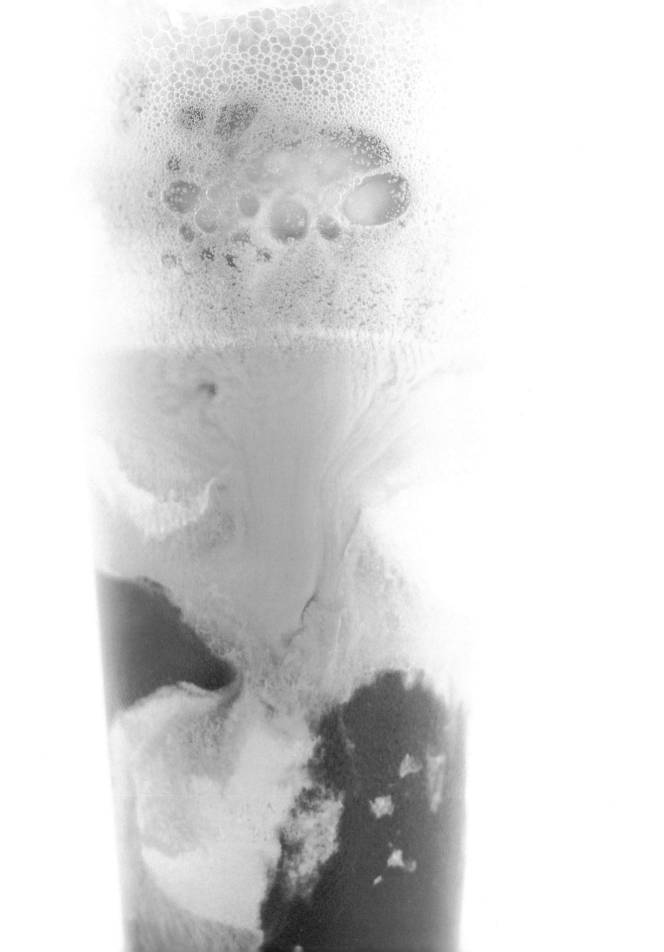

## useful addresses

These are some of my favourite suppliers.

**Amy Willcock:**
www.amywillcock.co.uk

*The George Hotel*
Quay Street
Yarmouth
Isle of Wight PO41 OPE
tel: 01983 760331

*Amy's range of textiles, Chic Kit*
ICTC
tel: 01603 488019
www.ictc.co.uk

*Amy's range of cookware, Rangeware*
Mermaid
tel: 0121 554 2001
www.mermaidcookware.com

**Food:**
*The Soil Association*
tel: 0117 314 5000
www.soilassociation.org

*National Association of Farmers' Markets*
tel: 0845 230 2150
www.farmersmarkets.net

*Daylesford Organic Farm Shop*
Moreton-in-Marsh
Gloucestershire GL56 OYA
tel: 01608 731700
www.daylesfordorganic.com

*The Healthy Way*
30 High Street
Ilfracombe
North Devon EX34 9DA
tel: 01271 865 883
www.healthy-way.co.uk
Fantastic peanut butter.

*L Robson & Sons*
Craster
Northumberland NE66 3TR
tel: 01665 576223
www.kipper.co.uk
Craster kippers.

**Cheese:**
*La Fromagerie*
2–4 Moxon Street
London W1U 4EW
tel: 020 7935 0341
www.lafromagerie.co.uk
Cheese, spices and tea.

**Bakery:**
*Poilâne*
46 Elizabeth Street
London SW1
tel: 020 7808 4910
www.poilane.com
You can freeze their breads very successfully – I always bring home bagfuls of bread in the car.

*Treacle*
160 Columbia Road
London E2 7RG
tel: 020 7729 5657
www.treacleworld.com
They are only open on Sundays but it is worth the trip to buy cakes for the week ahead.

*Ladurée*
16 rue Royale
750087 Paris
www.laduree.fr
Great macaroons that freeze well.

**Cookware:**
*E Dehillerin*
18–20 rue Coquillere
Paris
www.dehillerin.fr

*Divertimenti*
227–229 Brompton Road
London SW3 2EP
tel: 020 7581 8065
www.divertimenti.co.uk

*Bake-O-Glide*
tel: 01706 224790
www.bake-o-glide.co.uk

**Glass and china:**
*William Yeoward*
020 7351 5454
www.williamyeowardcrystal.com

*The Dining Room Shop*
62–64 White Hart Lane
London SW13 0PZ
tel: 020 8878 1020
Fantastic things for dining!

*Emma Bridgewater*
tel: 020 73719077
www.bridgewaterpottery.co.uk
Do also have a look at Emma's husband's site, Matthew Rice, for fab calendars, place cards and notebooks.
www.matthewrice.co.uk

*Thomas Goode*
tel: 020 7499 2823
www.thomasgoode.co.uk

*Mary Howard Sales*
tel: 01386 700850
www.maryhowardsales.co.uk
Mary's sales are legendary – they are a must! You can buy anything and everything for home and self!

**Undercloths for wooden tables:**
*John Lewis*
tel: 020 7828 1000
www.johnlewis.com

**Candles:**
*Wind Light*
Tolsey House
Bull Ring
Ludlow
Shropshire
tel: 01584 878444

**Antique Mirrors:**
*Jane McNeile Decorative Antiques*
tel: 020 7587 0353
jane@mcneile.com

**Flowers:**
*Covent Garden Flower Market*
New Covent Garden Market
London SW8 5NX
tel: 020 7720 2211

*Marianne Robic*
39 rue de Babylone
7th arrondissement
Paris
You will be inspired and it is a must!

*Flamant*
8 rue Furstenberg
6th arrondissement
Paris
www.flamant.com
This is a fantastic tableware shop and has a small florist as well.

*Tiger Rose*
Bridge House
West Meon
Petersfield
Hampshire GU32 1JG
tel: 01730 829989
www.tiger-rose.co.uk

**Domestic staff:**
*Beauchamp Bureau*
186 Sloane Street
London SW1X 9QR
tel: 020 7259 6999
www.beauchampbureau.co.uk

**Venues:**
*Blandings Country House Parties*
tel: 020 7947 3290

**Party goods:**
*Cox and Cox*
tel: 0870 442 4787
www.coxandcox.co.uk

*Confetti*
tel: 0870 840 6060
www.confetti.co.uk

**Food publication:**
*The Art of Eating*
www.artofeating.com
Brilliant American quarterly food magazine.

**Stationery and invitations:**
*Wren Press*
1 Chelsea Wharf
15 Lots Road
London SW10 0QJ
tel: 020 7351 5887
www.wrenpress.com

*Smythsons*
40 New Bond Street
London W1S 2DE
tel: 020 7629 8558
Menus, guest books, place cards, etc.

I would also recommend buying a copy of *Debrett's New Guide to Etiquette and Modern Manners* – it can help with the most mundane of questions, like what to do when the Queen comes to tea!
www.debretts.co.uk

## author's acknowledgements

The success of this book is due to many people, and I am indebted to them all for their support and critique. Huge thanks to Sarah Lavelle and the Ebury team, Jonathan Gregson, Gillian Haslam and Chris Wood – your support has been tremendous; Sarah Wooldridge and her team at IMG – a girl couldn't ask for better back-up; my recipe testers, Kevin Mangeolles and all at *The George*; Louise Mackaness; Mike and Zannie for Miss Mini; Gwen for the loan of china; Champagne Taittinger for keeping us merry throughout the photo shoots; Catherine and Jo who keep the home fires burning; and last but not least my family, Jeremy, Jo, John, Harriet and Charlotte. Thank you!